TERMINATING PUBLIC PROGRAMS

TERMINATING PUBLIC PROGRAMS

An American Political Paradox

With a foreword by
Senator William V. Roth, Jr.

Mark R. Daniels

M.E. Sharpe
Armonk, New York
London, England

Library of Congress Cataloging-in-Publication Data

Daniels, Mark Ross, 1952–
Terminating public programs : an American political paradox / by Mark R. Daniels
p.   cm.
Includes bibliographical references and index.
ISBN 0-7656-0124-9 (cloth : alk. paper).—ISBN 0-7656-0125-7 (pbk. : alk. paper)
1. Political planning—United States—Evaluation.
2. Policy sciences—Evaluation.
3. Public administration—United States—Evaluation.
4. Sunset reviews of government programs—United States. I. Title.
JK468.P64D36   1997
320'.6'0973—dc21   97-10553
CIP

Printed in the United States of America

The paper used in this publication meets the minimum requirements of the
American National Standard for Information Sciences—
Permanence of Paper for Printed Library Materials,
ANSI Z 39.48-1984.

♾

BM (c)   10   9   8   7   6   5   4   3   2   1
BM (p)   10   9   8   7   6   5   4   3   2   1

To Dr. Patrick J. Fett

Contents

Tables and Figures

Foreword

Thirty years ago, as a freshman Congressman, I undertook a project to examine the size and scope of the Federal government. A committed proponent of balanced budgets, tax cuts, and a limited bureaucracy, my objective was to compile a list of all the federally operated programs providing assistance to the American public.

Little did I know how massive and challenging that project would be. As my staff and I made countless telephone calls, searched government manuals, Federal Registers, and Congressional Records, as we wrote letter after letter, and even searched the government-listings pages of public telephone books, we discovered two things: first, that it would be impossible to know exactly how many Federal programs are in existence; and, second, that forces within the government itself did not want such a list compiled.

As I said the day I introduced the "Roth Study" on the floor of Congress, my staff and I found that the Federal government itself did not possess enough information on all its programs to allow our study—which took eight dedicated months—to assemble a comprehensive list. We found that there was not enough information for the Federal government to make even reasonable comparisons of one program with another, or to prevent costly and inefficient duplications.

We found many instances where cabinet departments and agencies had programs devoted to the same general activities—and that there was no way to cross-reference them, no way to compare the programs side-by-side in a meaningful manner that would allow us to examine them, to cut away those programs that were needless and streamline those that were useful and productive.

Again, this was thirty years ago. The Federal budget was $178 billion. Today total annual outlays are over $1.6 trillion. The government has mushroomed, despite repeated attempts to staunch its rate of growth or even to cut it back.

In the 1980s, Ronald Reagan appointed Peter Grace to chair his Private Sector Survey on Cost Control. Findings by the "Grace Commission" suggested that the conditions we had discovered over a decade earlier had become exacerbated. After trying to find out how many government programs exist, Peter Grace discovered that "no one had the answer. There is just no central source for that kind of information, which would be immediately available to any private-sector executive." Like us, Grace found that "the Federal government doesn't know how many offices it has or where they're located." The commission's best guess was that there were over 963 federal social programs alone.

One of the reasons for this explosion in government is the phenomenon that Professor Mark Daniels examines in *Terminating Public Programs*. Once created, a government organization is "virtually immortal." And when the rare organization is terminated, its functions are "usually transferred to another organization." In other words, while the government continues to grow—creating policies, roles, functions, and organizations to meet current and genuine needs—old policies, roles, functions, and organizations are not terminated, despite the fact that they, as most often is the case, are no longer necessary.

I realized just how absurd this condition had become when, as Chairman of the Senate Governmental Affairs Committee, I sponsored the legislation that created the bipartisan Military Base Closure Committee. Until that time, there had been no mechanism to effectively close military bases, despite how obsolete they had become, and the results were almost comedic. The purpose of one active base we looked at had been to serve as an outpost for the Pony Express. Another base in the South was actually protected by a moat. But as with any government program, these bases had their constituencies, their local communities that depended on them for economic reasons, and their Representatives and Senators to protect them in Washington, D.C.

The Military Base Closure Committee is one example of how innovative ideas can produce successful results. I am honored that this bipartisan effort is included in Professor Daniels's examples of programs that have worked. But I am troubled that his list of successful terminations is so short. It means that there are countless other public programs, policies, and organizations that are no longer vital to the well-being of America, or that do not contribute in the manner for which they were originally intended. Yet they continue to exist because of inertia, because of protectionist measures by their patrons in Congress and the Executive Branch, or, as Professor Daniels demonstrates, due to their sheer bureaucratic strength.

Beyond the Military Base Closure success, there have been a few other important steps in the effort to make the Federal bureaucracy more efficient and cost-effective. For example, in 1993, Congress passed the Government Performance and Results Act, which requires Federal agencies to develop five-year strategic plans with measurable long-term goals. The law also requires annual performance plans and reports on whether or not those plans are achieved. GPRA was a critical step toward establishing performance-based management and assessing the mission, value, and success of Federal agencies.

But it was only a step.

There is growing bipartisan consensus that the era of big government is over. Even a casual look at demographics and economic trends shows that the Federal government of the future will need to have fewer agencies and a smaller cabinet. Each department will need to be organized around tightly focused, national priority missions. Redundancies, for economic reasons alone, will need to be eliminated. We cannot afford otherwise, and technology will allow government to do more with less.

In my mind, our government for the twenty-first century will have a streamlined field structure and offer something like "one-stop shopping" where Americans and our small businesses can be served in a single office. I see a government with a new breed of "operating units" where administrative systems are customized to meet the unique needs of their programs—where a new class of non-political managers are hired on long-term performance contracts—and where those managers are held accountable for the results they achieve.

With this book, Professor Daniels makes an invaluable contribution to the realization of such a future. As he makes clear, "terminating policies is necessary in order to free up resources for new policies," and "political leaders need to know more about termination if restructuring government is on top of the policy agenda."

Terminating Public Programs provides us with a concise, readable, and thought-provoking tool in this important effort. It brings into one volume a comparison of case studies about termination and offers a comprehensive review of literature relevant to the topic. While these alone are necessary resources in our effort, Professor Daniels also provides a detailed examination of the obstacles to terminating needless government programs, and gives his reader what can be considered a blueprint for success. Of particular interest to me are the steps that must be taken for policy and organizational termination that he outlines in chapters two and six.

Not long ago, Peter Drucker wrote that "Any organization, whether biological or social, . . . needs to rethink itself once it is more than forty or fifty years old. It has outgrown its policies and its rules of behavior. If it continues in its old ways, it becomes ungovernable, unmanageable, uncontrollable."

This is where our Federal government is today. We cannot afford to remain here long.

Our government must change. Old and needless programs and policies must be abolished to make way for government that is innovative, efficient, and cost-effective. Departments, agencies, and management paradigms built for the industrial age must be reinvented for the information age.

In this effort, as Professor Daniels says, "political leaders . . . will find themselves facing tough termination decisions." Those who succeed will be, as Drucker suggests, those who have thought through in advance what needs to be done. *Terminating Public Programs* is the kind of advanced thinking we need. I laud the research and recommendations this book provides to a debate that is becoming more important to Americans, and to our future.

The Honorable William V. Roth, Jr.
United States Senator, Delaware

Preface

My interest in policy termination began while I was in a doctoral seminar conducted by the late Professor Frank K. Gibson at the University of Georgia. I was Dr. Gibson's graduate assistant, and he requested that I copy the symposium on policy termination published in the journal *Policy Sciences*.[1] Later in class, Dr. Gibson called upon me to define and present some of the key terms and concepts involved in policy termination. Fortunately for me, I had read the symposium. I remember being extremely fascinated by the topic, especially in the light of how overlooked it had been in policy studies. After completing my Ph.D., I subsequently required my public affairs students at the University of Connecticut to read and discuss this symposium.

Much later, in 1993, a case study I was writing about Oklahoma's experience closing the State Training Schools seemed to illustrate some of the obstacles to termination. I soon found myself searching through the termination literature. Chapters in a book written by Garry Brewer and Peter deLeon, *The Foundations of Policy Analysis*,[2] provided an excellent orientation, examples of cases, and a bibliography about termination. This in turn led me to reread two public policy classics, *Are Government Organizations Immortal?* and *Time, Chance and Organizations: Natural Selection in a Perilous Environment*,[3] both written by Herbert Kaufman. I found myself hooked on the policy termination literature and over the next five years I wrote three articles[4] and a book chapter,[5] and edited a symposium in the *International Journal of*

Public Administration[6] on termination. This book is the end result of my efforts to understand further and draw conclusions about policy termination.

There are many people I want to thank for assisting me with this project. First, Professor Frank K. Gibson created an interest and fascination within me for public policy research. I will always remember his seminars at the University of Georgia and often think back to his teaching style and his interpersonal skills with students as a role model and guide for my own teaching and student interaction. His memory remains a source of inspiration and guidance for me.

Second, I want to thank Professor Peter deLeon of the Graduate School of Public Affairs, University of Colorado at Denver. Dr. deLeon has provided substantial comments and advice not only on this manuscript but also while serving as a referee and author in the *International Journal of Public Administration* symposium on termination. His time and attention and his recommendations are deeply appreciated.

Third, I want to thank Professor Herbert Kaufman, whose comments and suggestions on this manuscript have helped greatly my understanding and appreciation of his work in this field. Professor Kaufman's research analyzes the phenomenon of organizational death, which is a much narrower focus than that taken in this book. Those researchers who extrapolate Professor Kaufman's theory of organizational death to programs and policies do so, of course, on their own initiative. I thank Dr. Kaufman for his time, attention, and correspondence.

Fourth, two young gentlemen, Nathaniel and Noah True-Daniels, deserve my special thanks for the patience they have shown as sons of a struggling author and professor. Hearing their voices in the background while writing has been a source of comfort and security for me rather than a distraction. Nathaniel and Noah have helped me discover the true meaning of life.

Lastly, I dedicate this book to my dear friend and colleague, Dr. Patrick J. Fett. His brave reticence in the face of cancer humbled all who knew him. I have never known a colleague to equal his honesty, kindness, humor, and playfulness. He was an authentic intellectual, a respected teacher, and an irreplaceable human being.

Of course, I take exclusive and full responsibility for any errors, misinterpretations, or misapplications within this book.

TERMINATING PUBLIC PROGRAMS

1

Public Policy and Organization Termination: An Overview

The B-1 strategic bomber was one of the greatest and costliest airplanes ever designed. Compared to its predecessor, the 1950s era B-52, it could take off from shorter airstrips and fly at supersonic speeds. Its short take-off capability allowed for easier deployment at military airbases around the world, and its supersonic speed would make interception harder for enemy missiles and fighters. In addition, it had digital, electronic terrain-skimming instruments that allowed it to fly at ground level, a low radar profile, and high bomb-load capacity. Even among air force fighter pilots, who are usually reluctant to fly the slower, cumbersome bombers, the B-1 was a hot ride.[1]

In 1973 the American Friends Service Committee decided to organize a nationwide, grassroots network of volunteers to oppose the further development of the B-1 bomber. They did so for a number of reasons, such as continuing the antiwar movement even after the Vietnam Peace Treaty, to protest the destruction caused to Vietnam by B-52 bombings, to expose the role of corporations in profiting from weapons systems, and to protest the cost to taxpayers of paying for the B-1. The American Friends eventually had a thousand local organizers and fifty campaign offices throughout the nation. They would organize demonstrations on special occasions and hold vigils outside Internal Revenue Service offices.

On the other side of the issue was Rockwell International, the primary contractor of the B-1. Rockwell made sure that the funds spent on the plane would be channeled through subcontractors in forty-seven states, ensuring that almost every U.S. senator and representative had constituents who would be adversely affected by any funding cuts on the plane.

The most important accomplishment of the American Friends' protest was making the B-1 an issue in the 1976 presidential campaign. Not only did candidate Jimmy Carter oppose the further funding of the bomber, but the Democratic party's Platform Committee labeled the B-1 a waste of taxpayers' money. The price of the B-1 fleet in 1973 was $53 billion and increased to $90 billion in 1976. Meanwhile, in the U.S. Senate, Democrat John Culver of Iowa proposed a budget amendment to delay funding of the bomber until 1977, allowing the next president ultimately to decide the B-1's fate. Culver's amendment was tabled, but an amendment was proposed by Senator William Proxmire that delayed a funding decision until 1977 but allowed funding to continue on a month-to-month basis. The Proxmire amendment was approved, and one year later newly elected President Jimmy Carter terminated the B-1 bomber program and replaced it with the Cruise missile program that would use the aging B-52s as launch pads.

The story of the B-1 sounds like a successful scenario of how to terminate a government program. A $90 billion defense program that relied on subcontractors from across the nation is killed by a group of volunteer Quaker pacifists, along with help from a newly elected president and some political "friends" in the U.S. Senate. This is perhaps democracy at its best: a grassroots network composed of ordinary citizens taking on Rockwell International, the epitome of the military-industrial complex.

In reality, the death of the B-1 is an excellent termination example simply because the B-1 did not remain dead for long; it was raised from the dead as a result of the election of President Ronald Reagan in 1980. Reagan campaigned to restore funding to the B-1, and by 1981 the first operational B-1s were being constructed. This time around, the B-1s would be equipped with Cruise missiles, thus retaining Carter's defense spending initiative and restoring funding to the B-1. The case of the B-1 demonstrates a government termination phenomenon: there is usually life after death for terminated government programs.

The almost uncanny ability of public organizations and their programs and policies to survive and prosper in the face of political and legal efforts aimed at their demise has led former Yale University professor and Brookings Institution scholar Herbert Kaufman to ask, "Are government organizations immortal?"[2] Although public organizations and policies are human creations and are certainly not immortal, they are hard to end, kill, terminate. Like Dr. Frankenstein's monster, the creation eventually defies the creator. Yet despite the unsuccessful results that politicians have had terminating public policies and organizations, a common campaign theme has always been to eliminate bureaucracy and cut government down to size, at least to the size it was a quarter or a half century ago. Before examining current efforts by political leaders to terminate government policies and organizations, termination itself needs to be defined. The next sections advance a definition of termination, locate termination within the public policy process, explain the most common reasons for termination, and clarify the different types of termination.

Defining Termination

Public policy scholars Garry Brewer and Peter deLeon define public-sector termination as "the deliberate conclusion or cessation of specific government functions, programs, policies, or organizations."[3] Termination is premeditated behavior, with the intent of ending a particular public organization or policy. This definition does not recognize changes in policy emphasis or jurisdiction, which may be organizational attempts to redirect activities and to justify existence, as policy termination.

Brewer and deLeon's definition also does not apply to cutback management, which is an attempt to reduce the size or scope of an organization or policy in the face of substantial budget cuts.[4] Similarly, government downsizing, which shifts programs and policies from one government organization to another, or from one level of government to another, is also not included in this definition of termination unless the actual elimination of programs, policies, and organizations is involved.[5]

Termination is the conclusion or ending of a government program, policy, or organization. It is not merely the adjustment of an organization to a smaller budget or the shifting of government services to a private-sector contractor.

Termination and the Public Policy Process

Policymaking is a continuing process moving from the perception of problems needing a government response to formulating, implementing, and evaluating the adopted policies.[6] As part of the policy process, termination occurs at the very end, as a last step. Garry Brewer and Peter deLeon identify six steps in the policymaking process: initiation; estimation; selection; implementation; evaluation; and, finally, termination.[7] Charles Jones similarly identifies seven steps in the policymaking process: getting problems to government attention; formulating proposals; legitimating programs; budgeting programs; implementing programs; evaluating programs; and last, conclusion, resolution, termination.[8] In both cases, termination is seen as the final outcome of a political, but highly rational, policy process. Seen this way, termination is an integral part of the American political process. Usually, however, termination has been treated as not so much an end as a beginning: a beginning to correct an errant policy or set of programs or to revise programmatic assumptions or components.[9] Termination in both these treatments of steps is not so much a deliberate end to a policy or program as it is a revision or readjustment.

Reasons for Termination

Peter deLeon examined numerous termination experiences and concluded that there are three main criteria, or reasons, leading to termination decisions: financial imperatives; governmental efficiencies; and political ideology.[10] Huge budget deficits and tax revenue shrinkage lead to financial imperatives: programs are reduced wherever such cuts are deemed politically possible. Governmental efficiencies also revolve around cost and performance issues: is a program too costly in terms of service delivered? For example, the Comprehensive Employment and Training Act (CETA) was terminated when the excessive cost of training employable personnel was discovered. Lastly, some programs are terminated without regard to financial imperatives or efficiencies and solely on the basis of political ideology. For example, President Nixon's opposition to the Office of Economic Opportunity and President Reagan's opposition to the Departments of Energy and Education were based upon ideological reasons.

In addition to the three reasons listed by deLeon, a fourth reason can be advanced: a change in behavioral theory about how administrative, human, or social services should be delivered. For example, health research conducted during the 1950s demonstrated the behavioral benefits that deinstitutionalization gave to mental patients. Although opponents of institutionalization often dramatized abuses in mental institutions in order to rally the public behind reform efforts, their objective was the creation of health services more appropriate and effective for treating mental illness. Other health care reforms have also stressed organizational and policy termination.[11]

Finally, a fifth reason for termination also exists. Robert Biller suggests that termination is "critical to learning."[12] That is, given the change and uncertainty that characterizes modern postindustrial societies, and given policymakers' limited ability to forecast the future appropriateness or success of current policies, terminating policies that do not work is one way for policymakers to learn from their mistakes. Biller suggests that policymaking should be initially carried out on a trial basis, with "short time and money tethers," and that policies should be corrected and adjusted according to feedback mechanisms. Although there are few examples of trial-type policymaking, the social experiments of the 1960s conform to this type of termination. For example, the New Jersey Negative Income Tax experiment tested an innovative approach to public assistance, representing a reform of the U.S. welfare system. The program was implemented on a sample population, ended after only a few years, and provided economists and social scientists with valuable data about welfare system alternatives.

Types of Policy Termination

The termination of public programs and policies has so far referred to the end of government functions and organizations in addition to programs and policies. At times, it is not possible to differentiate between a program and its government organization or its government function. As an example, deLeon points out that the Social Security Administration (SSA) as an organization is difficult to distinguish from its publicly funded, government-administered pension function, or from its social security payments program.[13] Terminating the SSA as an organization also means terminating the function and program of public pension administration. Nonetheless, it is possible to distinguish among the termination of a public function, organization, program, or policy.

A government function is defined by deLeon as a service provided by the government that transcends organizations and policies.[14] Functions are essentially services that the public has defined as within the common interest and that would not be delivered, or would be impossible to deliver, if not delivered by the government. Given that functions are tied to underlying assumptions about the role and responsibility of government, functions appear to be the most resistant to termination.[15]

Organizations are defined by deLeon as groups of employees that constitute a governmental institution, and the existence of organizations is closely tied to the government functions they provide.[16] Organizations are virtually immortal, but they are easier to terminate than functions. When organizations are terminated, the function they perform is usually transferred to another organization.[17]

Policies are general approaches or strategies applied to the performance of government functions and are much more susceptible to termination due to four reasons identified by deLeon.[18] First, organizations usually act out of self-preservation and will sacrifice a policy in order to save the whole. Terminated policies can always be replaced with new policies that employ different approaches or strategies. Second, policies have fewer allies in the policy arena than does an organization. Organizations usually have stronger political supporters than do policies. Third, policies are easier to isolate and evaluate than organizations, which may have multiple policy objectives. Fourth, organizational critics usually focus their complaints against particular policies, which can be sacrificed in order to save the organization. Policy termination, as opposed to functional or organizational termination, has so far been the predominant level of analysis for policy termination analysts.

Finally, programs are the easiest targets to terminate. As operational manifestations of policies, programs are the primary focus of investigators and can easily be dropped and replaced with other, "more effective" programs if need be.[19]

It may be useful to see these four types of policy termination as a hierarchy, arranged from the top down, from the most resistant to termination to the most susceptible to termination (see Figure 1.1). Government functions are most resistant to termination, followed by organizations, policies, and finally programs, which are most susceptible to termination.

Figure 1.1 **Termination Resistance Hierarchy**

Most Resistant

Functions

Organizations

Policies

Programs

Least Resistant

Termination's Current Political Popularity

The 1994 congressional elections returned control of both houses of Congress to the Republican party for the first time in forty years. It was also the first time in 130 years that a sitting Speaker of the House was defeated for reelection. Much of the credit for this astounding Republican victory was given to a document entitled "Contract With America."[20] This document presented a wide range of policies that would be implemented if voters returned control of Congress to the Republicans. The policies listed in the Contract are based on five principles: individual liberty; economic opportunity, limited government; personal responsibility; and security at home and abroad. All Republican congressional candidates pledged to uphold the Contract if elected.

One of the proposals in the Contract is a balanced budget amendment, along with a line-item veto. The balanced budget amendment would take effect in fiscal year 2002, and the line-item veto as soon as possible. According to the Contract, "balancing the budget will not be easy. It will require a fundamental restructuring of government. We believe the American people are ready for government that does less of the wrong things, but does the right things well."[21]

The line-item veto would allow the president to veto specific parts of a budget submitted by Congress without vetoing the entire budget. According to the Contract, "the President should have line-item veto authority to single out unnecessary and wasteful spending provisions in bills passed by Congress."[22] The line-item veto would give a "President—Republican or Democrat—the authority to cut wasteful pork-barrel spending."[23]

This is tough talk. Balancing the budget by 2002 would require hundreds of billions of dollars in spending cuts. But the Contract did not identify what specific programs, policies, or organizations would be terminated by such cuts. Although the Contract spoke of "doing less of the wrong things" and eliminating "wasteful spending," no specific programs were identified as either wrong or wasteful. For example, the Aid to Families with Dependent Children (AFDC) program was slated for reform, but not termination. The Contract called for prohibiting AFDC payments to unmarried mothers under age twenty-one, requiring paternity be established to receive AFDC, and freezing annual spending growth to 3.5 percent. These reform conditions would probably result in less spending for the program, but not its termination. Again, termination is not cutback management, and spending less on AFDC would not mean its demise.

The Contract also suggested that state governments should be able to choose to withdraw from the AFDC program, convert their payments into a fixed annual block grant, and use the payments to fund their own family aid programs. If these new state-offered family aid programs were significantly different from AFDC, and at the same time still met federal mandates for the block grant money, this could be considered a termination of AFDC in those applicable states. But for those states that retained the federal AFDC program, merely shifting program responsibility for AFDC from the federal to state governments does not sound the death knell for AFDC. While these suggested changes would result in a restructuring of government, or at least the AFDC part of government, they would not necessarily result in the termination of the AFDC program.

In their book *Reinventing Government*, David Osborne and Ted

Gaebler also offer many ideas about restructuring government.[24] Many of their suggestions involve decentralizing government and making government more responsive to the community, more customer service oriented, and more results oriented. None of these suggestions are linked to specific plans for terminating government policies or organizations. During their discussion about making government more market oriented and having government program administrators compete with private contractors, one gets the impression that some of these government programs would be terminated and put out of business. But the authors never explicitly state that certain government programs would be terminated by competing in the marketplace with private-sector contractors.

Osborne and Gaebler also discuss plans for making government smaller, as does Vice-President Al Gore in his book *Creating a Government That Works Better and Costs Less*.[25] Part of this plan requires laying off unnecessary government workers. According to Osborne and Gaebler, "governments are like fat people who must lose weight. They need to eat less and exercise more."[26] They suggest that the number of "useless personnel" in federal agencies is somewhere between 25 and 50 percent, and examples abound in both books about what Osborne and Gaebler call "trimming" and "paring payroll." These authors do not call for the termination of specific organizations or programs; however, the human resource reductions they call for would almost require the death of certain programs. At the same time, these authors suggest that services traditionally delivered by government should be taken over by nongovernment organizations (NGOs) that would employ nongovernment workers to deliver public-interest-oriented services. There would be substantial layoffs, government organizations would be terminated, but laid off workers could find employment in the new NGOs.[27]

Some specific organizations have been terminated. A very recent example is the military base terminations recommended by the bipartisan Military Base Closure Committee. Termination scholar Peter deLeon has identified the recent death of the Congressional Office of Technology Assessment, and the scheduled death of the National Institute of Standards and Technology.[28] During the Reagan administration, the 1978 Airline Deregulation Act resulted in the termination of the Civil Aeronautics Board, and the Comprehensive Employment and Training Act died a natural death when its authorization was allowed to lapse in 1982.

Despite the vagueness with which it is discussed, cutting the federal government and getting rid of federal programs are popular themes in current political discourse. But while the rhetoric of termination is enjoying a current popularity, the termination of a government program, policy, or organization is rare.

Eugene Bardach observed in 1976 that "termination occurs—when it does occur—with either a bang or a very long whimper."[29] In the former case, public programs and policies end, after a lengthy resistance, with a shattering force. A lengthy political struggle finishes with an explosive ending. With the latter case, public programs and policies end after a long-term decline in the resources with which a program or policy is sustained. In either case, the key phrase in Bardach's quotation may be "when it does occur"—referring to the reality that program or policy termination continues to be rare. And, as Bardach has also observed, "it is precisely the rarity of the phenomenon that makes it important."

Termination remains as rare in the 1990s as is was in 1976 when Bardach made his observations. Given the current popularity of cutting the size of government and doing away with public programs, the rarity of termination makes it an even more elusive topic. Political leaders need to know more about termination if restructuring government is on top of the policy agenda.

The Study of Public Policy and Organization Termination

The academic study of termination is almost as rare as the number of government programs actually terminated. While the earliest study of public-sector termination occurred in the 1950s, it was not until the 1970s that termination received serious attention.[30] In 1976, Eugene Bardach edited the first symposium on policy and organization termination and included in his introduction generalizations about how and why termination occurs, and what obstacles to termination exist.[31] The symposium contained eight original research articles exploring different aspects of termination. Since that time, fewer than fifteen termination manuscripts have been published, only one public policy textbook includes termination as a distinct topic, and only two books have been published on this topic, both by the same author.[32] What accounts for the paucity of termination studies?

Peter deLeon observes that " . . . termination is never an easy activity, even under conditions that would appear conducive."[33] In other words, relatively few studies of termination are written because there are relatively few cases of termination available for study.

A second reason for termination's neglect is that researchers prefer to focus on new, innovative policies, or new theoretical approaches to policy processes, rather than focus on ending outdated, flawed, or ineffective policies. There is little incentive to focus on old policies and ways of ending them, when attention is better received for studies that stress new policy development.

A third reason for the dearth of termination studies is that policy termination is a difficult intellectual topic. For example, many public programs experience "drift" or a change in program goals or components across time. At what point does a program drift so much that the program no longer resembles the original? At what point does drift become termination of the original program? The difficulty of operationally defining the concept of termination, which would allow examining termination as a separate policy field, has discouraged many potential researchers.

Conclusion

Despite the difficulty that public administrators and political leaders have had in terminating public policies and organizations, termination has emerged as a politically popular topic and enjoys substantial debate. Cutting bureaucracy, getting rid of obsolete public programs, and reinventing and replacing government are themes of contemporary campaign slogans and political discourse. Despite its current political popularity, termination has received very limited study over the past twenty years. In sum, the study of policy and organization termination has been and continues to be, in the words of Robert Biller, a "wrongly underattended issue."[34]

The chapters that follow conduct a comprehensive analysis of policy and organization termination in order to understand why policies or organizations are terminated, how they are terminated, and what often prevents them from being terminated. Attention will be given to identifying theories of termination that have been tested and supported by research.

Chapter 2 reviews the research conducted on termination with special attention to several theories that have been applied by a variety of researchers to analyze actual termination experiences. These theories have been found very useful in explaining and understanding termination. Chapter 3 presents a unique termination approach, Sunset legislation. A review of Sunset includes findings and judgments about how well Sunset has performed as a termination mechanism. An analysis is also conducted to establish whether or not the termination of policies is linked to developing and adopting new policies.

Chapter 4 presents the case of terminating Oklahoma's Public Training Schools. This case demonstrates how policies can continue even though specific programs and organizations have been terminated. Chapter 5 examines the relationship between the study of implementation, or the actual carrying out of public policy, and the termination of policy. Insight is provided on what steps need to be taken in order to carry out, or implement, termination successfully.

Chapter 6 summarizes the overall findings of this book and offers suggestions, based on the termination research studies examined in the book, to political leaders and public administrators on what obstacles and outcomes to expect when engaged in termination activities.

2

The Literature of Termination

One shortcoming of research conducted on policy termination is that it usually takes the form of a single case study that in some way is idiosyncratic. As Eugene Bardach observed, because "social science—and social scientists—thrive on generalizations rather than idiosyncracies, termination has never become 'hot' as a topic of academic interest."[1] Although never a "hot" topic, termination has nonetheless been a subject of intermittent study over the past few decades. This chapter reviews the research conducted on termination and pays special attention to theories that have been applied to actual termination experiences.

The 1976 *Policy Sciences* Symposium

Eugene Bardach edited the first collection of termination studies in a special issue of *Policy Sciences* in 1976.[2] Bardach's introduction to the symposium was the first attempt to generalize about how and why termination occurs, and what obstacles to termination exist.

Bardach, editor of the symposium, wrote the lead article, "Policy Termination as a Political Process."[3] In his article, Bardach argues that termination is actually a special case of policy adoption: the adoption of policy A requires the elimination or curtailment of policy B. The uniqueness of this form of policy adoption lies in the vested interests who oppose the termination of policy B.

Bardach observes that when termination does occur, it does so with either a bang or a very long whimper.[4] In the former case, resistance to the termination of policy B is so intense that when it finally does occur it does so in an abrupt, forceful fashion. In the latter case, termination occurs as a result of a long-term decline in the organizational resources that supported policy B.

Advocates of termination, Bardach explains, fall into three categories. First, the Oppositionists, who want the policy terminated because they see it as flawed or bad. Second, the Economizers, who are concerned about reallocating resources from the terminated program to another program. And, third, Reformers, who see the termination of one policy as an opportunity to adopt new, better policies.

Bardach believes that there are five reasons why termination is rarely attempted. First, when policies are developed they are designed and given the resources to survive for a long time. When a policy is selected for termination, the terminators soon find out that the policy has substantial resources with which to survive. Second, policy termination often involves a brutal fight between supporters and terminators. These are fights most politicians wish to avoid. Third, termination is rarely attempted because political leaders do not wish to admit that earlier decisions they have made have become mistakes. Fourth, termination may not only end a program but may also result in employees being laid off and a reduction in government spending within a certain legislative district. Terminators are reluctant to end a currently existing program at the expense of damaging the apparatus of the program. Fifth, Bardach believes that there is simply a lack of political incentives for terminating programs.

What conditions facilitate policy termination? The first condition Bardach identifies is a change in administrations. This results in political participants who are not tied down to past decisions. A second condition is an ideological opposition to particular institutions. For example, an antitechnology ideology resulted in the termination of the Supersonic Transport plane in the early 1970s. Third, a period of political turbulence often gives political leaders an opportunity for reorganization. A fourth condition is ameliorating the effects of the termination. For example, arranging for the continued employment of personnel employed by a terminated program within another government program cushions the blow of termination. Finally, the fifth condition is designing a policy for eventual termination once specific program goals have been achieved.

Robert P. Biller's article "On Tolerating Policy and Organizational Termination: Some Design Considerations" argues that the question is not whether a policy or organization should end, but rather where and when and under what circumstances it should end.[5] Terminating policies is necessary in order to free up resources for new policies. If a policy has solved a public problem or task, then it should be terminated because it is no longer needed. If it has not proved itself to be a solution, then it should especially be terminated in order to make available resources for replacement policies that may be more successful. Exploring alternative policies and programs in pursuit of the public interest by definition requires and expects the termination of programs that have run their course. Biller advances an internal matrix design for public policies that would allow for their eventual demise. This matrix design includes both bureaucratic and market-based approaches to public service. The more programmatic work of public service could be accomplished through bureaucracy (for example, highway maintenance), while less programmatic work would be the task of temporary policies and organizations (for example, job training programs during an economic recession, similar to New Deal programs). While the bureaucratic policies would have a permanence attached to them, the market-based programs would exist only as long as they were needed.

Robert D. Behn's article "Closing the Massachusetts Public Training Schools" examines the termination of the Public Training ("reform") Schools as a way of examining a successful policy termination.[6] Behn's primary research question was how Dr. Jerome G. Miller, commissioner of the Department of Youth Services, was able to accomplish what so few others have: terminate a government program.

Starting in the 1960s, state governments began a trend by closing state-operated Training Schools. These were actually "reform" schools, intended for delinquent youth. For example, the Massachusetts Division of Youth Services (DYS) removed nearly 1,000 delinquent youths from state training schools and placed them in an array of community-based services. Reformers argued that closing the schools was supported by research, which found that large juvenile facilities do not deter crime and often create violent and antisocial behavior among residents.

Behn first identifies five survival tactics used by administrative agencies listed in a public administration textbook and looks at how Dr. Miller was able to overcome these tactics and terminate the schools.[7] The first tactic is seeking the support of important extragovernmental groups. Commissioner Miller did not have any direct client or organized interest group to contend with. He did, however, have the employees to consider, and anticipating the confrontation that would result from layoffs, Miller decided to remove the youths from the schools but leave the employees on the payroll. Although forty-four employees were eventually terminated, Behn observes that "the willingness of Miller . . . to leave unproductive DYS employees on the payroll while the institutions were closed and the policy changes consolidated was essential to neutralizing the resistance of the employees."[8]

The second tactic is seeking legislative support. Miller received the legislative support of the House Speaker, and though he received some criticism for some administrative practices, there was never any legislative movement to reopen the schools. When Miller found it difficult to obtain state funds from the legislature, he avoided the need for legislative support and instead accessed federal funds from the Law Enforcement Assistance Administration, administered through the governor's office.

Seeking the support of superiors and other persons of prestige is the third survival tactic. One of the biggest supporters for school reform was the governor's spouse, Jesse Sargent. With the support of the governor, key staff members of the governor, and Jesse Sargent, Miller was able to rely on prestigious allies. At no time did Miller's superiors question his discretion or decision making.

The fourth tactic is seeking public support. Miller was successful in obtaining public support. As Behn notes, Miller "changed the political question from 'What do we do with these bad kids,' to 'What do we do with these bad institutions?' "[9] He made sure that the public realized and understood the need for reform in the schools.

The fifth, and last, survival tactic is executive compromise and survival. Miller did not originally want to close the schools. Instead, he wanted to "replace the 'custodial model' of the reformatories with the 'therapeutic community model'—to 'humanize' the institutions."[10] After his efforts to retrain the staff failed, Miller decided to close the institutions rather than deal with staff resistance to retraining. He put the staff in the unenviable position of either supporting the closing or defending the existing inhumane system. Once his efforts to retrain the staff failed, he eliminated any compromise with the staff over reform issues by closing the schools.

Behn also studies how the termination of the schools was implemented. He refers to three problems of implementation identified by Jeffrey L. Pressman and Aaron B. Wildavsky and examines how Commissioner Miller avoided them: changing actors, diverse perspectives, and multiple clearances.[11] First, the actors involved in closing the schools did not change, with "most of the major political figures . . . involved during the entire critical period."[12]

Second, Behn believes that of the diverse perspectives identified by Pressman and Wildavsky only "legal and procedural differences" was a real problem for Miller.[13] There were many administrative rules and regulations outside his span of control, which prevented Miller from spending funds on the projects he desired and from assigning loyal personnel to the tasks he wanted done. For example, when faced with a shortage of funds for a special camping program at the Middlefield school, he named the program an "annex" of the Shirley school, located seventy miles away, and used funds from the Shirley budget for the Middlefield program. As Behn describes, "Miller employed as elastic and creative interpretations as possible" in order to ensure prompt and successful implementation.[14]

Third, Miller and his staff faced obstacles resulting from multiple clearances and approval requirements but circumvented barriers, went outside regular administrative channels, and used high-ranking executives to walk paperwork through the bureaucracy. While no criminal wrongdoing was committed, staff members admitted to not following state procedures in the quest to implement reform. Behn concludes that closing the Massachusetts Training Schools was successful because Commissioner Miller did not separate the initiation of policy termination from the implementation, the actual "carrying out," of policy termination. Miller skillfully negated the survival tactics of the status quo system of training schools and outmaneuvered the obstacles to termination by acting quickly and creatively. In a later article, Behn outlines a dozen "hints" for anyone planning to terminate a policy or organization based upon Massachusetts' successful experience closing the training schools (see Table 2.1).[15]

Mitchel B. Wallerstein's article "Terminating Entitlements:

Table 2.1

Robert Behn's One Dozen Hints for Policy and Organizational Termination

Hint 1:   Don't float trial balloons
Hint 2:   Enlarge the policy's constituency
Hint 3:   Focus attention on the policy's harm
Hint 4:   Take advantage of ideological shifts to demonstrate harm
Hint 5:   Inhibit compromise
Hint 6:   Recruit an outsider as administrator/terminator
Hint 7:   Avoid legislative votes
Hint 8:   Do not encroach upon legislative prerogatives
Hint 9:   Accept short-term cost increases
Hint 10:   Buy off the beneficiaries
Hint 11:   Advocate adoption
Hint 12:   Terminate only what is necessary

Veterans' Disability Benefits in the Depression" relates the formidable opposition to congressional attempts to reduce or limit entitlement benefits.[16] Wallerstein demonstrates how difficult it is to kill a "sacred cow" government program in the face of a well-mobilized, clearly identifiable constituency.

This theme continued with Abram N. Shulsky's article "Abolishing the District of Columbia Motorcycle Squad."[17] The motorcycle squad was formed in 1926 out of a concern for traffic safety. Police officers continued to serve on the motorcycle squad almost fifty years later, despite a substantial increase in crime and a relative decrease in traffic deaths. Efforts to eliminate the squad were initially successful, but the motor patrolmen were able to lobby the U.S. Congress and mobilize public opinion, and the squad was brought back to life in a slightly modified form. This case not only confirms Wallerstein's findings about how hard it is to terminate a program with a mobilized, clearly identifiable constituency but also demonstrates how terminated programs often have a life after death.

One article in the symposium clearly demonstrated what Bardach previously referred to as the "whimper" of termination: the death of a program resulting from the slow decline of resources that sustained it. W. Henry Lambright and Harvey M. Sapolsky in "Terminating Federal Research and Development Programs" assess the chances of killing such programs and conclude that the best strategy is "decrementalism," or slowly reducing funding to a point where the program is essentially dead.[18] This slow, measured approach to termination helps to avoid the opposition by constituency groups that would certainly occur if the program was abruptly terminated.

Valerie J. Bradley's article "Policy Termination in Mental Health: The Hidden Agenda" demonstrated the disastrous effects of terminating an old, outdated program without providing for the development of a new replacement program.[19] Mental health reformers during the 1960s successfully closed the large state institutions for the mentally ill that generally provided inadequate and at times inhumane care for the patients. However, the decentralized, community-based programs that were intended to replace the large institutions fell victim to efforts by state governments to shift fiscal responsibility to local governments. For example, when the governor of California, Ronald Reagan, simultaneously closed the state mental institutions and cut back state funding for providing outpatient services, the burden of caring for the patients fell on local governments. Quite often, these patients could not be accommodated by limited local mental health services and subsequently received no services at all. Bradley's study emphasizes the need for "pairing" program development objectives with program termination objectives.

Finally, James L. Foster and Garry D. Brewer contemplate an agenda for research on the termination of war in their article "And the Clocks Were Striking Thirteen: The Termination of War."[20] Their discussion of the termination of the Vietnam War is consistent with the "decrementalism" earlier referred to by Lambright and Sapolsky. Vietnam definitely ended with a whimper, not a bang.

While this symposium was noteworthy for its ground-breaking studies of termination, it apparently did little to stimulate the further study of termination. With the exception of Behn's refinement of his termination framework, the symposium did not stimulate researchers to conduct additional research in this field. Instead, termination research over the next two decades was conducted by only a handful of authors.

Herbert Kaufman and Organizational Death

Herbert Kaufman first explored the concept of organizational death in his book *Are Government Organizations Immortal?*, followed some years later with the book *Time, Chance, and Organizations.*[21] Kaufman views organizations as similar to, but not the same as, living organisms. If organizations were similar to living organisms, then organizations should have a life cycle of "youthful vigor, maturity, old age, and death."[22] Death, or the termination of an organization, should be a natural consequence eventually resulting from the birth of an organization. Kaufman finds, however, that unlike living organisms, organizations experience birth and maturation but rarely death. The relative absence of death distinguishes the organizations from the life cycles of other organisms and prevents the portrayal of organizations as living organisms.

In his first study, *Are Government Organizations Immortal?* Kaufman surveyed ten of the eleven executive departments in existence in 1973 in the Executive Office of the President and compared the number of organizations listed in a 1923 Brookings Institution study of the federal administrative structure. Kaufman was examining the life cycles of the organizations: how many births over a fifty-year period; how many deaths; and the number of birthdays, or age, of the organization. He found that of the 175 organizations that existed in 1923, only 27 were terminated over a fifty-year period, or about 15 percent. Kaufman then examined the mortality rate of private organizations over the same fifty-year period by looking at business failure statistics and found that private organizations had a death rate over two times higher than public organizations. Why do public organizations have a greater life expectancy?

Kaufman suggests that the marginal change provided by an incremental government decision-making process insulates governmental organizations from a natural life cycle. Those deaths that did occur seemed, to Kaufman, to be attributable more to chance, or bad luck, than to any other factor. For most of the terminated governmental organizations studied by Kaufman, "overall, however, chance seems to have played a large part in their termination."[23] The question "are government organizations immortal?" is asked as part of the conclusion of the study.

The immortality of organizations was further pursued in his *Time, Chance, and Organizations*. In this study, Kaufman hypothesizes that organizations die because "the inflows of energy and other resources necessary for them to keep their activities going, to keep their engines running, dry up."[24] It is in this work that he advances his notion of organizational development as a type of evolution. Organizational death is the failure of systems maintenance, the inability of an organization to evolve and adapt to new environmental conditions: organizations no longer adapt to their environment; fall behind the evolution of other, more successfully adapting organizations; and eventually go the way of the dinosaurs. Kaufman continues, however, to regard chance as playing a role in the termination of organizations: the timing of termination, not the existence of organizational death itself, appears to be random, left up to chance, the luck of the draw.

Kaufman's work measures the resiliency of government organizations and suggests that much more study is needed before generalizations can be made about which organization, under what circumstances, and at what time, will become terminally ill. A hypothesis that Kaufman advances for testing is the "threshold test." According to this hypothesis, "organizations form out of a medium consisting of people, culture in the fullest sense, and energy; and the medium is enriched, or 'thickens,' as a result of the activities of organizations—even when organizations dissolve, for their contents return to the medium and are recycled to other organizations."[25] Kaufman is making an organic comparison that as living things are formed out of the "dust" of the planet, so too are organizations formed out of the medium of people. The medium out of which living things are formed becomes thicker when the number and complexity of the ingredients comprised within it increases with time. With organizations, as the activities and interdependencies of people multiply, and the levels of knowledge and skill rise, the medium that gives birth and sustenance to organizations becomes thicker.

The thickness of an organization influences how healthy and resilient it is to terminal diseases: an organization's thickness determines its resistance to termination. As an organization is developing over its life cycle—that is, as its medium is becoming thicker—it develops an ever increasing resistance to termination. Termination potential may be greatest just after birth, while an organization's medium is beginning to develop thickness, or after maturity, when an organization's medium may become static and inflexible and incapable of integrating new inputs or of producing enough maintenance outputs. Kaufman proposes seven factors as indicators of the thickness of an organization's medium (see Table 2.2).[26]

Kaufman's termination studies are both empirical and speculative. His data in *Are Government Organizations Immortal?* were from a

---

Table 2.2

Herbert Kaufman's Indicators for Thickness of an Organization's Medium

1. Organizational specialization: a high division of labor among organizations results in high interdependence and exchange.

2. Occupational specialization: a diverse, experienced workforce, possessing occupational expertise, can move from one organization to another without difficulty.

3. Literacy and educational levels: the extent of educational expertise, coupled with support from educational institutions.

4. Cultural institutions and personnel: the extent that research centers and libraries support organizations and share collective knowledge.

5. Volume and speed of communication: the means of storing, retrieving, sharing, and communicating the collective knowledge of the organization.

6. Energy consumption per capita: a high rate is a result of a technologically advanced organizational environment.

7. Organizational density: the greater the number of organizations, the greater the chances that complex combinations of organizations will form.

---

federal executive agency, and his conclusions were based upon statistical, summary analysis. In *Time, Chance, and Organizations*, however, Kaufman engaged in speculation about the nature of organizational existence and survival. Some reviewers expressed disappointment over what they perceived as the "speculative nature"[27] or the "overly sketchy comments"[28] of the book. In all fairness to Kaufman, however, his earlier work pioneered empirical inquiry into organizational death, and it was from this work that hypotheses about the development and evolution of organizations emerged. His work in *Time, Chance, and Organizations* is an effort at theory building and is designed to encourage more empirical research into organizational death.

Keith Mueller tested Kaufman's theory of organizational death by analyzing the repeal of the 1974 National Health Planning and Resources Development Act.[29] Mueller found that health planning survived for two decades because of the environmental support that provided life-sustaining resources for the agency. Health planning met the requirements advanced by Kaufman for agency longevity: it was created by legislative initiative; it was defended by powerful members of Congress; it had a relatively small budget; it had strong support from professional associations; and it had few critics. During the mid-1980s, however, the Reagan administration introduced competing legislation, key positions on congressional subcommittees were filled with opponents, a dominant and hostile interest group emerged, and the program was identified for elimination by the Reagan administration as part of budget reductions. Mueller found that because health planning could not adapt to this changing environment and the reduction of its resources, it soon exhibited Kaufman's organizational death symptoms and eventually died.

Richard Chackerian has applied Kaufman's theory of organizational death to the reorganization of state-level executive branches of government.[30] As Chackerian explained, because reorganization occurs only occasionally, the analysis of state government reorganization required an empirical method that takes time into account. In addition, the analysis also required a conceptual theory that was sympathetic to the importance of time: Kaufman's theory of organizational evolution and decline proved to be very useful. Chackerian found that large-scale state government reorganization occurred about every twenty-five years, with only a 3 percent chance of occurring in any one specific year. He concluded that his data supported Kaufman's theory that government organizations are more immortal than private organizations, although they are not absolutely immortal when viewed over a lengthy time period (in this case eighty-five years).

Chackerian was not able to provide a direct link between societal or economic events and state government reorganization. Just as with termination, reorganization occurs in cycles across time, but the actual timing or causal factors behind it cannot be isolated. Chackerian concluded that how the meaning of events is interpreted involves an extremely subtle process. Social and economic events are given meaning over time, and eventually political leaders may perceive that the time has come for a government reorganization.

This subtleness may provide the mystery behind the timing of termination. The interaction of social and economic events over long periods of time changes the medium in which an organization thrives and eventually, if the organization cannot respond adequately to this changing medium, the organization becomes terminally ill and dies. However, this interaction over time may be so subtle as to escape the detection and measurement by researchers. Thus, termination may seem to rely only on chance: what cannot

Table 2.3

Peter deLeon's Six Termination Obstacles

1. Intellectual reluctance: people do not like to consider that the underlying thinking behind a policy is flawed or is no longer relevant. People have a vested interest in the ideas behind policies.

2. Institutional permanence: organizations and their policies are designed to endure beyond a single sponsor or bureaucrat. This bureaucratic strength works against termination efforts.

3. Dynamic systems: organizations and their policies are systems that respond to and change with their environment. In this case, an organization or policy can always be one step ahead of termination.

4. Antitermination coalitions: significant political groups, some quite unsuspected, can arise in opposition to termination.

5. Legal obstacles: in a litigation-prone political environment, the guarantee of due process may postpone termination indefinitely.

6. High start-up costs: the notion that there are sunk costs that would be lost with termination often justifies the continuation of a suspect policy.

be adequately measured and predicted seems to occur only by chance over time.

Peter deLeon and the Politics of Termination

Peter deLeon hypothesizes that there are six reasons why policy termination may be difficult to carry out (see Table 2.3).[31]

One recent research project has tested deLeon's termination obstacles framework in an attempt to find patterns and generalize about policy termination factors. The first study, conducted by Janet Frantz, reviewed the efforts to terminate the U.S. National Leprosarium (renamed the National Hansen's Disease Center), which needlessly incarcerated and segregated victim's of Hansen's disease (HD) for their entire life, contrary to scientific research that found HD to be the least contagious of all infectious diseases.[32] Frantz questioned how such a flawed policy survived for so long, and found deLeon's termination hypotheses provided a useful model.

Most recently, deLeon has investigated to what extent terminations occurring during President Reagan's administration have been guided by cost/benefit types of economic analyses and evaluations.[33] He found that economics was rarely behind the decisions to terminate agencies or programs. For example, after the 1978 Airline Deregulation Act eliminated the need for the Civil Aeronautics Board (CAB), the CAB began to prepare itself for termination by reducing its staff from 830 to 351. At the same time, however, CAB's budget was reduced by only 25 percent. Another example given by deLeon is the proposed termination of the Department of Energy (DOE), which originally was justified through potential savings of $1.3 billion. Over time, the estimated savings shrunk to $1 billion, then to $250 million, and finally DOE Undersecretary Fiske admitted that the termination of the agency was not "being done because there is a cost savings of this much or that much."[34]

DeLeon's discussion builds on research conducted by James M. Cameron on the deinstitutionalization of California's mental health system.[35] Cameron defines ideology as "fixed conceptual principles unrelated to specific, contextual variables."[36] These principles can be political, social, or economic assumptions about what governments should do, and how they should do it. Because these principles are general assumptions, they are not linked to specific, ongoing policies or programs. Cameron reasons that since these principles are not related to specific programs, then they cannot be empirically proved or disproved, and "negative consequences flowing from the actual operation of policy are not linked to the controlling ideas."[37] Cameron examined the ideology behind the state mental hospital movement of the nineteenth century and the more recent community mental health movement and found that the current deinstitutionalization trend is a result of a changing ideology about mental illness and treatment. Closing state mental hospitals in California had a devastating effect on the morale of hospital personnel, resulted in the indiscriminate transfer of patients from one hospital to another, discharged patients into communities that were not prepared to care for them, and resulted in patients living a "lonely, isolated, alienated existence."[38] Cameron concludes that a changing ideology was behind the deinstitutionalization of California's mental hospitals, and empirical findings about the lack of clinical or economic justification for the closings did not change the termination decision. To the extent that principles such as "decentralization" and "deinstitutionalization" become guiding ideologies behind public policies, specific programs may be terminated without regard to cost-benefit or cost-effectiveness considerations.

DeLeon's most recent termination research suggests that policy termination is a result of political rather than analytical decision making and that political values and ideology are the main determinants of termination decisions. DeLeon's opinion is that fundamental questions of values and ideologies, rather than economies and efficiencies, provide the grounds for termination.[39]

The 1997 *International Journal of Public Administration* Symposium on Termination

Twenty years after the first symposium on termination, a second collection composed of five essays on termination will be published in volume 20 of the *International Journal of Public Administration*.[40] These essays all build upon the previous literature of termination, especially the work of Kaufman and deLeon.

Samuel Best, Paul Teske, and Michael Mintrom examine the death of the Interstate Commerce Commission (ICC) in their article, "Terminating the Oldest Living Regulator: The Death of the Interstate Commerce Commission."[41] They conclude that while the ICC's termination is consistent with many commonly mentioned reasons for termination, termination theory as it currently exists cannot explain when an agency will be ended. As Kaufman also observed, the timing of termination might well be a more difficult question than the termination itself. These authors suggest that two approaches from the policy change literature can provide insight into the timing of termination. These authors also suggest that a period of disequilibrium, during which an organization's support systems become more and more unstable, may be necessary to terminate an agency fully.

In the second article, "The High Cost of Policy Termination," Janet E. Frantz analyzes the costs of termination and concentrates on the termination of the hospitals of the Public Health Service.[42] She concludes that cost savings is rarely a reason for termination and that most terminations actually result in short-term cost increases.

Justin Greenwood examines the termination of programs in the United Kingdom during the 1980s and 1990s in an article entitled "The Succession of Policy Termination."[43] He finds substantial support for deLeon's termination framework but suggests that many terminations may actually result in policy succession, or replacement policies at a later date. As an example, Greenwood discusses the termination of a behavior-control program that provided membership cards for fans attending football matches: although the program was ended, crowd control was implemented through other mechanisms. Greenwood calls for further attention to the concept of "life after death" for many terminated programs.

In the fourth article, "Policy Termination: Uncovering the Ideological Dimension," Michael Harris examines the attempt of the Israeli government to terminate the failing kibbutzim (collectives) in the face of severe budget constraints and the realization that some kibbutzim would never be financially self-supporting.[44] Even though the political power of the kibbutzim continued to decline, the ruling Labor government would not abandon its support for them. The ideology of the kibbutzim, linked with the socialist/humanist ideals of the Labor party, was an obstacle to termination regardless of financial imperatives. Again, deLeon's model proves useful in understanding this case study.

In the final article, "Organizational Termination in the Nonprofit Setting: The Dissolution of Children's Rehabilitation Services," Dorothy Norris-Tirrell selects the termination of a nonprofit agency and applies deLeon's framework and Kaufman's life-cycle theory to her analysis.[45] She finds support for both these theoretical frameworks and introduces a new factor especially critical for analyzing nonprofit termination experiences, the importance of the selection of decision makers with competencies appropriate for the given life-cycle stage of the organization.

Peter deLeon concludes the symposium with an essay assessing the state of termination research in view of the research findings of the symposium articles and commenting on the current political atmosphere within which termination is discussed.[46] DeLeon observes that termination presents us with a paradox: the public wants services it cannot afford. As an example, he refers to a CNN/USA Today poll indicating that 88 percent of those polled want to balance the federal budget while a full two-thirds want tax cuts.[47] The public wants to balance the budget and cut taxes as long as these dramatic reductions in federal spending do not cut programs that directly affect them. For example, federal agricultural subsidies should be cut, but not if it affects products grown in my state; military spending should be cut, but not if it closes down the air force base in my community; the B-2 Stealth bomber should be cut, but not if it results in unemployment in my community. In deLeon's words: "In a polyarchic democracy, one in which multiple representations rule the roost, policy termination becomes a distant trumpet, always for somebody else, even when that 'somebody' cannot be identified."[48]

The paradox of policy and organization termination is that everyone is for it, as long as it does not affect him or her personally. Despite the overwhelming support for a balanced budget, there were many families with reservations to vacation at Yellowstone National Park in November 1995, who were very upset when the park was temporarily shut down as a result of the budget battle between Congress and President Clinton. Balance the budget if you must, but please do not ruin my vacation.

Conclusion

This chapter has reviewed the research conducted on policy and organization termination, and several theories emerge as useful in explaining the phenomenon of termination. First, recent studies conducted by Frantz and by Norris-Tirrell have found the termination obstacles framework developed by deLeon to be a useful model. Second, Kaufman's life-cycle model has been supported by several studies conducted by Mueller, Chackerian, and Norris-Tirrell. A third termination model developed by Behn proved useful in explaining the demise of Massachusetts' Public Training Schools.

However, the main characteristic of termination research is its paucity: within the past twenty years, only two symposia have appeared on termination and only a handful of books have addressed the subject. The next three chapters respond to the paucity of termination research by further exploring why policies and organizations are terminated, how they are terminated, and what often prevents them from being terminated. Chapter 3 will present the case of Sunset legislation, a termination tactic used by many state governments. The discussion of Sunset legislation includes an exploration of the linkages between termination and policy innovation.

Chapter 4 tests the theories of deLeon and Kaufman by examining the termination of Oklahoma's Public Training Schools. Finally, Chapter 5 applies Behn's implementation framework to the termination of Tennessee's Medicaid program.

3

Sunset Legislation: Exploring the Linkages Between Termination and Innovation

Termination is the ultimate adjustment of people, policies, programs, systems, and institutions that have ceased to work well. Death, divorce, bankruptcy, election recall, the repeal of legislation, and even revolution can be seen as examples of termination. But even as life continues through birth, so too are people remarried, businesses recapitalized, freshman representatives elected, new laws passed, and sovereignty established for new governments. The sense of finality that coincides with termination gives way to a spirit of rebirth and creation.

As authors Garry Brewer and Peter deLeon have observed, "termination signals a beginning of the policy process as much as it does its end."[1] The idea that termination frees up resources for new policies and programs has also been advanced by Robert P. Biller. Termination is critical, explains Biller, because the death of policies and organizations creates "space" that provides recycled resources that can be used for alternative policies.[2]

As policies mature and grow old over time, they continue to address public problems that may have already been resolved, have changed drastically in nature or intensity, or have possibly been surpassed in importance by new problems perceived to possess greater social importance and priority. Ending outdated policies releases economic and administrative resources that can be applied to new problems through innovative policies. As Brewer and deLeon observe, a current challenge facing most modern societies is how to adapt policymaking attitudes and habits developed during periods of high and sustained economic growth to the changing political and social demands resulting from economic stagnation.[3] Perhaps a government's capacity for pursuing innovative policies during periods of economic stagnation is most dependent upon its capacity for terminating outdated government organizations, policies, and programs.

This chapter advances and tests the theory that a government's capacity for adopting innovative policies depends on its ability to terminate outdated organizations, policies, and programs. Related hypotheses are tested focusing on the governments of the continental American states, the adoption and application of Sunset legislation, and the associated policy innovativeness of these states.

Sunset Legislation and the Federal Government

Despite many efforts at budgetary reform, federal budgeting remains an incremental process in which the most important factor in deciding an agency's budget is the amount of the previous year's budget. Legislators look only at additions, or increments, when a new budget is formulated, and last year's programs continue to receive funding with little or no review. In 1976, Senator Edmund Muskie (Democrat, Maine) introduced a legislative method designed to eliminate incremental budgeting: the so-called Sunset Act.

The Sunset Act carried with it the assumption that every federal program will automatically terminate unless there is a vote to continue it.[4] Incrementalism would be replaced with a performance evaluation of each federal program before continued funding would be approved. Under the Muskie bill, federal programs would be reviewed once every eight years. Implicit in Sunset legislation is the threat of termination. As Robert D. Behn explains: "the objective is to replace the assumption that every program automatically continues unless there is a vote to terminate it, with the assumption that every program automatically terminates unless there is a vote to continue it."[5]

Despite its promise of budgetary reform, Sunset legislation never was approved by Congress. Critics felt that the work involved in reviewing all federal programs would create tremendous pressure on administrators and might result in evaluations conducted in a superficial fashion. In addition, agency evaluations would be conducted by congressional oversight committees, the very legislative bureaucracies that are biased in favor of the continued funding of the agencies. In the end, no one on Capitol Hill believed that the Internal Revenue Service, the Federal Bureau of Investigation, or the Federal Aviation Administration would actually be terminated. Instead, programs with low funding and weak constituencies would probably be the targets of termination, and if these agencies were meant to be terminated they could be so even without Sunset legislation.

Although Sunset legislation never was adopted by the federal government, many state governments viewed Sunset as one of the most significant legislative movements of the 1970s.

Sunset Legislation and the State Governments

Sunset legislation is designed to terminate agencies and boards of state government automatically. Its intent is not so much to provide an immediate end to state agencies but rather to require state legislators to conduct comprehensive program evaluation of existing boards and agencies.[6] Nonetheless, six years after the first state adopted Sunset legislation, a total of 271 boards and agencies were terminated, and numerous others were reorganized, re-created, or consolidated.[7] As of January 1989, a grand total of 325 state government entities were terminated.[8]

Since the enactment of the first Sunset law by Colorado in 1976, a total of thirty-six states have adopted Sunset laws (see Figure 3.1).[9] The review cycle of state agencies and boards is specified by some Sunset laws, and can range from every four to every twelve years. The objectives of most states adopting Sunset laws was to improve agency efficiency and accountability. The automatic termination mechanism was a very real threat that was meant to require legislators to conduct vigorous program evaluation. Common Cause conducted the first comprehensive survey of the impact of Sunset legislation in 1982 and found that the benefits of Sunset included improvements in government performance through increased agency efficiency and public accountability; financial savings, with one-sixth of Sunset states reporting sizable savings; and legislative experience in conducting oversight, especially in linking oversight to the normal legislative process.[10]

Figure 3.1 **Decision Process of Sunset Legislation** (n=50)

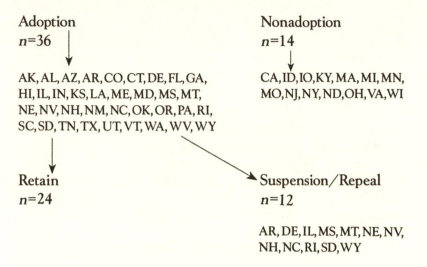

Adoption
n=36

AK, AL, AZ, AR, CO, CT, DE, FL, GA,
HI, IL, IN, KS, LA, ME, MD, MS, MT,
NE, NV, NH, NM, NC, OK, OR, PA, RI,
SC, SD, TN, TX, UT, VT, WA, WV, WY

Retain
n=24

Nonadoption
n=14

CA, ID, IO, KY, MA, MI, MN,
MO, NJ, NY, ND, OH, VA, WI

Suspension/Repeal
n=12

AR, DE, IL, MS, MT, NE, NV,
NH, NC, RI, SD, WY

Since 1976, according to Common Cause, nearly 1,500 state agencies have been reviewed under Sunset, starting with 15 agencies in 1976 and increasing to 500 agencies in 1981. Almost one in every five agencies reviewed has been terminated, once in every three modified, and less than half re-created with little or no change.[11]

The most recent survey and analysis of the American states' experience with Sunset was conducted by Richard C. Kearney.[12] Kearney reports that Sunset legislation has successfully terminated more than 325 state government entities. More importantly, he notes, "state executive branches have been cleaned up through the deletion of nonfunctional, redundant, or unnecessary entities."[13] Ironically, however, Sunset has led to the creation of new government agencies. For example, Florida has terminated 90 agencies under Sunset since 1978, but has created 104 new agencies. Despite its apparent success with state governments, Sunset is not without its problems. Some legislators had false expectations about the effects of Sunset, such as an instant reduction in the size of state government, or instant dollar savings from Sunset.[14] Common Cause concluded that many states underestimated the amount of time involved to evaluate or at least to review state agencies and programs. In addition, many states lacked adequate measurement information on agency performance and therefore could not make a quantitative cost-benefit assessment on the value of the agency. These problems led some states to repeal or suspend Sunset legislation.

Kearney reports that twelve states have repealed or suspended the enabling legislation.[15] While some of these states undoubtedly had experienced problems with Sunset, some of them actually had relatively successful experiences with the process. For example, Montana terminated 5 agencies, Connecticut 29, Arkansas 28, Rhode Island 17, New Hampshire 15, and Illinois 50 agencies. Kearney hypothesizes that the states repealing or suspending Sunset may have developed alternative legislative oversight procedures or have not been able to maintain Sunset review due to low levels of legislative professionalism. Kearney's quantitative, comparative analysis of the Sunset dropouts confirms that, with the exception of Illinois, the dropouts are characterized by weak legislative capacity for the type of intensive evaluation and review required by Sunset. Part-time legislators with weak professional staff assistance are hard pressed to complete the evaluation and review involved in oversight of the Sunset process.

Sunset legislation enacted by state governments provides an opportunity to conduct a comparative analysis of similar termination efforts by governments. The next section explores whether or not the termination efforts of state governments through Sunset lead to the adoption of new programs and policies.

Termination and Innovation

Measuring Termination and Innovation

An innovation is defined as an idea perceived as new by an individual.[16] It is an idea that is new to the individual adopting it, no matter how old the idea may be or how many other individuals may have adopted it.[17] In this respect, Sunset legislation is an innovation for each state that considers its ratification, no matter how many states have previously adopted Sunset.

Innovativeness is the adoption proneness of an entity that has the capacity for decision making. Jack L. Walker[18] explores the general tendency toward innovativeness of state governments and concludes, after examining 88 policies, that states have relative levels of innovativeness and that it is possible to attribute general innovative tendencies to state legislatures. Virginia Gray examines twelve policies and finds that state innovativeness often depends on the issue and time

Table 3.1

Correlations Among Innovation Scores

Gray	Savage	Walker
1.000	.6045	.7358
	P < .000	P < .000
	1.000	.5888
		P < .000
		1.000

Note: Spearman's rho coefficients

period characterizing the policy.[19] And Robert Savage, in the most comprehensive study, finds that innovativeness is a pervasive factor among the states, and that it is somewhat issue and time specific.[20]

Innovation scores have been calculated by several researchers. Jack Walker calculated innovation scores for the 48 continental American states based on the adoption pattern of 88 policies,[21] Virginia Gray calculated innovation scores based on 12 policies, and Robert Savage based his scores on 69 policies.[22] Ranking the states on each innovation index results in ordinal level data. Table 3.1 shows a correlation matrix for the ranks of the three innovation scores, and the high positive correlations indicate strong internal validity among the separate indices.

The first states adopted Sunset in 1976, and the highest number of states adopted in 1977.[23] In order to score the innovativeness of states on Sunset, ranks can be assigned based on the year in which Sunset was adopted (see Table 3.2). For example, states that adopted Sunset in 1976, the first year of adoption, are ranked one (1), states that adopted in 1977 are ranked two (2), and so forth until the last year of adoption, 1981, which results in a rank of six (6). Jack Walker assigned states that did not adopt a particular innovation the same score as states that were last to adopt the innovation. Robert Savage, however, assigned a rank to nonadopting states based on the year after the last state had adopted an innovation. This means that states not adopting Sunset as of 1982 are given the rank of seven (7).

Testing Termination and Innovation

If a government's capacity for adopting innovative policies depends on its ability to terminate outdated policies, the most innovative states

Table 3.2

Adoption of Sunset Legislation by Year

Year	States adopting	Rank
1976	AL, CO, FL, LA	1
1977	AK, AR, CT, GA, HI, ME, MT, NE, NH, NM,OK,OR, RI, SD, TN, TX, UT, VT, WA	2
1978	AZ, IN, KS, MD, SC	3
1979	IL, MS, NV, WV, WY	4
1980	DE	5
1981	NC, PA	6
	all other states	7

should be most active in policy termination. States that adopt Sunset legislation and are reviewing, revising, and often terminating previously enacted agencies and policies should also be the most active in adopting new replacement policies.

Three hypotheses are tested here to explore the relationship between Sunset review and policy innovation. First, states that adopt Sunset are more innovative than states that have not adopted Sunset. In order to test this hypothesis, the rank of states on the three innovation indices are statistically compared for adoption and nonadoption states.

A second hypothesis expects that states most innovative in adopting Sunset—those with lower adoption ranks—are also most innovative in adopting other policies. That is, the desire to embrace an automatic approach to termination is associated with an inclination to adopt new policies quickly. In order to test this hypothesis, the ranks of states on the innovation scores are correlated with the rank of the states on Sunset adoption.

A third hypothesis is that states repealing or suspending Sunset after initial adoption are less innovative than states retaining Sunset. In order to test this hypothesis, the ranks of states on the innovation scores are statistically compared for states that have repealed/suspended Sunset and those that have retained Sunset.

Table 3.3

Relationship Between General Policy Innovativeness and Sunset Legislation Adoption and Nonadoption

Rank on policy	States on Sunset (mean score)		
Innovation index	Adoption mean	Nonadoption	
Gray	16.57	27.76	P < .0118
Savage	18.82	26.84	P < .0713
Walker	15.71	28.12	P < .0083
	n = 34	n = 14	

Notes: Mann-Whitney U statistic; Two-tailed test.

Table 3.3 reports the results of testing the first hypothesis. There is a statistically significant relationship between general policy innovativeness and the adoption of Sunset legislation on two of the three innovation indices.[24] This falls short of demonstrating a causal relationship between the willingness to adopt a legislative termination mechanism and the tendency to embrace new public policies quickly. The results show only that Sunset-adopting states have a greater tendency toward policy innovativeness than nonadopting states. While this can be seen as a connection between termination and innovativeness, it can also be seen as further evidence that a state's general policy innovativeness reveals a willingness to adopt all new policies, including the policy of Sunset review. In this sense, Sunset adoption may not be so much an enactment of termination as it is an adoption of yet another new policy, another innovation.[25]

Table 3.4 reports the results of testing the second hypothesis. There is a statistically significant relationship between general policy innovativeness and the speed of Sunset legislation adoption. Unexpectedly, however, the relationship is inverse. States that quickly adopt other innovations are most reluctant to adopt Sunset. States that are usually slow in adopting other innovations, the "laggard states," are most innovative when it comes to adopting Sunset legislation. The speed of Sunset adoption is measured by a state's adoption rank: the speed of adoption and the order of adoption are the same. States that usually are slow in adopting other policies were among the early adopters of Sunset.

Insight about this inverse relationship can be obtained by referring to

Table 3.4

**Relationship Between General Policy Innovativess and the Adoption
Order of Sunset Legislation**

Rank on policy		Sunset adoption
Innovation index	Innovation rank	
Gray	−.3563	P < .013
Savage	−.0941	P < .525
Walker	−.3195	P < .027

Notes: Spearman's rho coefficients; $n = 48$

a study on legislative oversight conducted by Keith E. Hamm and Roby D. Robertson, which included a discriminant analysis of Sunset adoption and a number of independent variables that measured legislative professionalism.[26] These researchers found that low legislative professionalism, little party conflict, and a large administrative structure are most related to the adoption of Sunset laws. These findings suggest that Sunset review is most attractive to those state legislatures needing the greatest assistance with oversight. Adopting Sunset is a strategy of a weak legislature to exert power over the state bureaucracy and perhaps the governor. In Walker's ground-breaking study of policy innovation, the innovation scores of states strongly correlated with measures of party competition, legislative turnover, and legislative professionalism.[27] Innovative states possess highly professional legislatures, do not necessarily need to increase the capacity to conduct legislative oversight, and are therefore less inclined to adopt Sunset review quickly.

Regarding the third hypothesis, data analysis reveals no relationship between general policy innovativeness and repeal/suspension or retention of Sunset. Although Kearney found that weak legislatures have a tendency to repeal or suspend Sunset review, there is no evidence that these states are generally less innovative than states that retain Sunset.

Conclusion

Although Sunset was not adopted by the federal government, state governments embraced this termination mechanism with enthusiasm. But the substantial workload and lack of program performance measures have resulted in numerous states revising or rescinding Sunset. Although Sunset has resulted in the elimination of scores of state programs and agencies, it has not lived up to its expectations. As Maryland's Speaker of the House explained, "Sunset was oversold. We were looking for an easy solution. Sunset was something we could understand, and there were expectations that were too high."[28]

Is a government's capacity for adopting innovative policies dependent upon its ability to terminate outdated organizations, policies, and programs? After testing several hypotheses involving the relationship between the adoption by state governments of Sunset legislation and the states' general policy innovativeness, little supporting evidence for this theory has been uncovered. The results of this study, however, have provided additional insights about the nature of Sunset legislation.

Sunset legislation is an innovation for each adopting state. And, as an innovation, states that are generally innovative and that adopt other new policies are prone to adopt Sunset legislation. But states that are usually reluctant to adopt other new policies quickly, the "laggard states," are among the first on the Sunset bandwagon. The relatively low legislative professionalism of these states, and the inability of these legislatures to conduct oversight of public programs and agencies effectively, leads these legislatures to adopt Sunset as a means of strengthening their oversight function, and of obtaining greater power over the administrative bureaucracy and the governor.

Ironically, it is also this low legislative professionalism that has led some of the Sunset-adopting states to repeal or suspend Sunset. The substantial workload involved in reviewing agencies of state government is too much for part-time legislatures with little staff assistance.

During a period of economic stagnation, the termination of outdated policies can free up economic resources that can be used to create new policies that are more consistent with a recession economy. President Clinton's welfare reduction proposals coupled with new welfare initiatives, the closing of military bases accompanied by job training programs for former defense employees—these are all examples of how policy termination signals a beginning of the policy process as well as its end. Perhaps future testing of the relationship between termination and innovation should focus on a systematic assessment of cases on a national basis or on a comparison of termination and innovation activity on a particular policy area or problem shared by all states.

4

Organizational Termination
and Policy Continuation

This chapter examines the termination of Oklahoma's State Training Schools for dependent and neglected children in order to explore the usefulness of existing policy termination models. Guiding the analysis of this case are the termination theories of Peter deLeon and Herbert Kaufman, which were presented in Chapter 2. The first termination theory applied to this case is deLeon's obstacles to termination framework[1] and the second is Kaufman's theory of organizational medium thickness.[2]

Although the organization and bureaucracy of state training schools in Oklahoma ended, the policy of institutionalization—this time in psychiatric hospitals—continued. How a policy can continue, though ended in one organizational manifestation, through a different program in a different bureaucratic location, offers new insights into the obstacles of and prospects for policy termination.

The Death of Oklahoma's Public Training Schools

Abused and neglected by a mentally ill mother and an alcoholic father, Terry D. was taken away from his parents at age nine. After a series of unsuccessful placements in foster homes, he was declared by the State of Oklahoma to be a "dependent and neglected child" and was admitted to a state training (reform) school.[3] In 1978, when Terry D. was fifteen years old, a class action suit was filed in Terry's behalf by Steve Nozick, deputy director of legal aid of western Oklahoma. Eight juveniles, including Terry D., represented the class of dependent and neglected children living in state training schools. The suit was filed against Lloyd E. Rader, secretary of the Department of Human Services (DHS), the DHS, and the State of Oklahoma and alleged the abuse of more than 900 juveniles who were committed to state institutions but who had committed no crime. These "nonoffenders" were dependents of the state due to parental abuse or neglect and were institutionalized along with juvenile delinquents. The suit bore the name of Terry D.

Six years later, after a lengthy legal battle, U.S. District Judge Ralph Thompson decreed that deprived children or those needing psychiatric treatment cannot be placed in an institution for delinquents. Instead, the decree emphasized "placing a child in the least restrictive environment, such as a group home, preferably in the child's neighborhood," or in a foster parent's home.[4] The decree called for widespread reform in Oklahoma's juvenile justice system. Children like Terry D. would now be placed in neighborhood group homes instead of reform schools.

Prior to the Terry D. case, emotionally disturbed dependent children were referred to as "status offenders" and were institutionalized along with delinquent children. Half of the children held in the state detention centers or training (reform) schools had committed no crime.[5] The Terry D. case focused not only on the behavioral appropriateness of placing emotionally disturbed children with delinquents but also alleged that physical abuse and improper medical practices occurred regularly.

The Terry D. decree prohibited placing emotionally disturbed or deprived children in an institution for delinquents and emphasized placing a child in the least restrictive environment, such as a community group home. The decree additionally called for the deinstitutionalization of delinquents, except those judged guilty of violent offenses and for whom secure detention was necessary. Again, the use of community-based treatment was advocated for delinquents. Overall, the decree stated the goal for juvenile services should be to "achieve a safe, humane, caring environment with access to needed services that will provide for normal growth and development and allow youth to lead lives as close to normal as possible."[6]

The Terry D. case prompted the State of Oklahoma to reform its juvenile services system even before the 1984 decree. In 1982, the Oklahoma legislature passed House Bill 1468, which included sweeping reforms in the juvenile system.[7] Simultaneously, five state training schools were closed. Legislative action called for community-based services to replace the closed institutions.

Oklahoma's decision to switch from an institutional to a community-based model reflected a policy shift other states were experiencing. According to the Center for the Study of Youth Policy at the University of Michigan, the trend to close large juvenile institutions began in the early 1970s in Massachusetts.[8] The Massachusetts Division of Youth Services removed nearly 1,000 delinquent youths from state training schools and placed them in an array of community-based services.[9] Reformers argued that closing the schools was supported by research that found that large juvenile facilities do not deter crime and "often create violent and anti-social behavior among inmates."[10] Massachusetts became the model for community-based youth services.

In the early 1980s, Utah closed its only training school and reduced the incarcerated juvenile population from 350 to less than 60. Like Massachusetts, Utah shifted its resources into community-based programs and treatments. Like Oklahoma, Utah was pressured by a federal lawsuit over the conditions of its juvenile services.

At the same time Oklahoma was reforming its juvenile services, Louisiana, Colorado, Pennsylvania, and Oregon were also looking at community-based services. Each state reduced the number of youth in secure institutional settings and patterned the reformed community-based services after the Massachusetts and Utah programs.

Authorizing new programs through legislative initiative was not enough actually to implement these programs. Appropriation of funds was also needed to begin these reform programs, and unfortunately, authorization occurred just prior to a severe recession in Oklahoma's economy. "Although the bill contained some innovative ideas for the juvenile justice system, a serious deficit really emerged," according to John Selph, a Tulsa County commissioner. According to Selph, "we closed the institutions, but the community-based program wasn't adequately supported or funded."[11] Referring to the federal decree and the need for expanded juvenile services, Governor David Walters observed that "we blew up the juvenile justice system and never created a new one."[12] Without adequate funding for the authorized community-based services, and with the closing of the state's training schools, the juvenile system was hard pressed to implement the Terry D. court decree. It was difficult to find a placement within the juvenile system for emotionally disturbed dependent children. Because the training schools were closed, the state had to find a location to place dependent children.

"In Need of Treatment" Adjudication

Prior to Terry D., children who entered the juvenile system were categorized as "deprived," "status offenders," or "delinquents." In 1982, prompted by the Terry D. deliberations, children were categorized as:

1. Delinquents: those who have committed crimes and are in custody of the state.
2. Deprived: those who have been abused or neglected by their families.
3. In Need of Services: those who are beyond the control of their parents.
4. In Need of Treatment: those who suffer from emotional problems.

Part of the Terry D. decision was that a court hearing and judgment—an adjudication—would be used to judge a child as "in need of treatment" (INT). Included in this category was "any child who is afflicted with a substantial disorder of the emotional processes, thought or cognition which grossly impairs judgement, behavior or capacity to recognize reality or ability to meet the ordinary demands of life appropriate to the age of the child."[13]

Depending upon the category in which a child is placed, a different array of services was intended to be available. Community-based homes and foster care are services that all categories of children might receive. In addition, delinquent children may require commitment to a secure detention center for evaluation before receiving other services. The treatment objective for all children is eventual return to their parent's home. But because INT children are considered emotionally disturbed, it is assumed that they cannot be adequately treated by the juvenile justice system.[14] Once a judge hears evidence from medical witnesses that a child is emotionally disturbed, the child can be adjudicated INT, taken out of the juvenile justice system, and possibly committed to a psychiatric hospital. Only in the INT category can a child

Figure 4.1 **Oklahoma Youth Commitments** (fiscal years 1983–90)

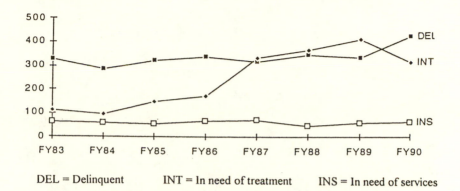

DEL = Delinquent   INT = In need of treatment   INS = In need of services

Source: Marty Beyer, Paul DeMuro, and Ira Schwartz, *Comprehensive Services for Oklahoma's Delinquent, Deprived, in Need of Treatment, and in Need of Services Children: Final Report* (Oklahoma City, Department of Human Services, State of Oklahoma, 1990), p. 8.

be taken out of the juvenile justice system and receive medical treatment for a diagnosed mental illness.

Some INTs are delinquents who have committed crimes. These children have been adjudicated INT and may be placed in a psychiatric facility instead of a secure detention center, a community-based home, or a foster home. Not all INT children have committed crimes or have been considered delinquent, however. All INT children are in need of mental health treatment due to abuse, neglect, or emotional or mental illness.

The deinstitutionalization of deprived children, status offenders, and delinquents was a major factor in the increase of INT adjudications. Figure 4.1 charts the commitments of children to state dependent custody, and the category in which the children were placed during the seven-year period from 1983 to 1990. Shortly after the 1984 INT adjudication decree, a steady and dramatic increase occurred in INT children. In 1987, more children were committed to state custody as INTs than as delinquents.

Most INTs were sent to hospitals. Table 4.1 gives the standardized percentages of INT placement in 1990. Medicaid considers residential treatment, psychiatric hospital treatment, and treatment in the Central

Table 4.1

Placement of INTs, 1990

	n	Percentage
Foster home	3	.5
Community home	46	6.0
Group home	221	29.0
COJTC/OYC15	156	20.0
Psychiatric hospital residential treatment	334	44.0
n =	760	100.0

Source: Beyer, DeMuro, and Schwartz (1990), p. 9.

Oklahoma Juvenile Treatment Center (COJTC) and the Oklahoma Youth Center (OYC) as inpatient treatment and eligible for payment. In this regard, 65 percent of all INTs received inpatient Medicaid reimbursed psychiatric treatment.[15] Of the remaining 35 percent, most were placed in group homes, with only a few placed in community or foster homes.

With the closing of the state training schools, and with the lack of adequate funding for community-based services, increasing numbers of children (delinquent or emotionally disturbed) found themselves adjudicated as INTs and committed to psychiatric hospitals. As a high-ranking official at the Oklahoma Department of Human Services (DHS) explained, "They're just called something else and put in psychiatric hospitals instead of the training schools."[16] According to psychologist Lois Weithorn, instead of "deinstitutionalized" these children were "trans-institutionalized."[17]

Given the 1983–85 recession in Oklahoma and the resulting loss of government tax revenue, inadequate funding for community-based services is understandable, if not justified. But given the lack of tax revenue for new community-based programs, where did and how could the state fund the cost of psychiatric care for INT children?

Medicaid and Juvenile Services

Medicaid pays for medical care of children who are dependents of the state or whose families are judged eligible for "indigent care" (medical care at government expense for low-income individuals). In 1989,

Table 4.2

Department of Human Services Percentage Change in Expenditures by Division (fiscal years 1982–89)

Division	Percentage
DCYS	+42
MR&DD services	+169
Rehabilitation services	+15
School for blind	+24
Deaf/hearing imprd	+05
Medical services	+93
Assistance payments	+35
Aging services	−17
Management info	+49
Teaching hospitals	+33
Disability determ.	+35

Source: Department of Human Services, State of Oklahoma, Annual Financial Reports FY1984 and FY1988.

Note: Capital expenditures not included, but does include state and federal funds.

DHS experienced a $125,502,000 deficit, of which Medicaid cost overruns accounted for $6,260,000, or about 40 percent.[17] Of DHS's FY1989 appropriation of $1,480,561,544, the largest expenditure area was the Medical Services Administration, which funds Medicaid. The Medical Services Administration received $710,867,357, or 48 percent of the DHS yearly budget. Medical Services expenditures have grown at a rate faster than almost any other DHS division. Table 4.2 shows the percentage change in expenditures by division for fiscal years 1982 to 1989. Medical Service expenditures grew 93 percent—almost doubled—in this seven-year period, second only to the 169 percent increase in Mental Retardation and Developmental Disabilities Services (MR&DD).

The increase in Medical Services expenditures is partially explained by the increase in the number of children who receive psychiatric services, which were paid for by Medicaid. Table 4.3 displays the number of individuals, age twenty-one and under, who received Medicaid-financed psychiatric care from 1982 to 1990. During this period, the number of admissions increased 581 percent, almost a sixfold increase.

Table 4.4 measures the cost of Medicaid claims paid for these admissions during the same time period. Expenditures rose 1,000

Table 4.3

Number of Minors for Whom Medicaid Paid Inpatient Psychiatric Facility Service

| Fiscal year | Total | Age of individual | |
		Under 6	6–20
1990	1,817	54	1,763
1989	1,541	31	1,510
1988	1,437	120	1,317
1987	1,111	60	1,051
1986	789	34	755
1985	868	73	795
1984	408	4	404
1983	441	5	436
1982	313	2	311

Source: Information taken from the Health Care Financing Administration Form HCFA 2082 as submitted by the Department of Human Services, State of Oklahoma, for years indicated.

Table 4.4

Costs of Medicaid Claims Paid for Inpatient Psychiatric Facility Services

| Fiscal year | Total | Age of individual | |
		Under 6	6–20
1990	$39,450,713	$855,196	$38,595,517
1989	41,219,770	466,667	40,753,103
1988	40,690,913	219,529	40,471,384
1987	27,162,867	213,185	26,949,682
1986	14,102,786	500,009	13,602,777
1985	13,677,329	647,284	13,030,045
1984	6,952,274	24,899	6,927,375
1983	7,227,540	32,507	7,195,033
1982	4,069,345	26,925	4,042,420

Source: Information taken from the Health Care Financing Administration Form HCFA 2082 as submitted by the Department of Human Services, State of Oklahoma, for years indicated.

percent, from slightly more than $4 million in 1982 to almost $40 million in 1990, a tenfold increase.

According to Peat, Marwick, Main and Company, an independent accounting and auditing firm, half of the top ten providers of inpatient hospital care ranked by total Medicaid payments in 1989 were

Table 4.5

Children's Psychiatric Hospitals Among Top Ten Providers of Medicaid Financed Hospitals (fiscal year 1989)

Facility	FY1989 payment
Central Oklahoma Juvenile Treatment Center	$4,880,542
Dillon Family and Youth Services, Inc.	4,030,355
Children's Medical Center	3,139,427
Oklahoma Youth Center	2,651,282
Christopher Youth Center	804,809
Total	$15,506,415

Source: Peat, Marwick, Main and Company, *Presentation to Oklahoma Department of Human Services Inpatient Hospital Reimbursement Study* (Chicago: Compass Consulting Group, 1989).

children's psychiatric hospitals. Table 4.5 lists these five children's psychiatric hospitals and the individual and grand total costs, rounded to the largest first dollar. These top five providers accounted for $15,506,415 of Medicaid funds spent for children's inpatient psychiatric services, or about 37 percent of FY1989 total expenditure of $41,219,770. Due to the availability of Medicaid funds for these services, some psychiatric facilities have developed a special business relationship with the State of Oklahoma for the treatment of INT children.

This costly intervention might be justified if inpatient treatment was judged most effective for aiding emotionally disturbed children. After a panel appointed by Judge Thompson investigated the use of psychiatric hospitals for treating INT children, however, a report was issued that concluded that over half the cases ended in treatment failure.[19]

Early in 1989, the U.S. District Court appointed a three-member panel to advise the State of Oklahoma about the types of juvenile programs needed to comply with the Terry D. decree. The report listed thirty recommendations to bring the state's juvenile system in conformity with the Terry D. decree.[20] The total price tag of the recommendations was about $40 million, or about how much the state spends each year admitting INT children to psychiatric hospitals.

Paradoxically, recession-blighted Oklahoma relied on the most costly and least effective intervention for treating emotionally disturbed children—psychiatric hospitals. While the federal court intended to end the policy of institutionalization, it instead only ended the program of operating state training schools. Despite the court's decision, the policy of institutionalization continued, this time through the use of admission to psychiatric hospitals.

Evaluating Hypotheses: Patterns and Generalizations

What additional insights into policy termination result from the examination of Oklahoma's deinstitutionalization experience? First, intellectual reluctance was advanced by deLeon as an obstacle to termination. Here, the intellectual reluctance of the Oklahoma legislature to adopt or even consider children's mental health or juvenile justice reform resulted in using psychiatric hospitals as the new program manifestation of the policy of institutionalization. Unlike the Massachusetts experience discussed in chapter 2, where training schools were closed under the initiative of the Department of Youth Services in favor of alternative community-based group homes, Oklahoma had no alternative programs to replace the dead training schools.[21]

Abolishing inappropriate reform schools and saving taxpayers' money is desirable, but replacing an ineffective, costly policy with nothing is how Oklahoma's juvenile system became involved with psychiatric hospitals. For example, Representative Linda Larason of Oklahoma City introduced House Bill 1544, which called for the elimination of the INT procedure. Larason reported that her measure would save state Medicaid money and end inappropriate treatment.[22] Although it passed 94–4, a companion bill, which required an annual state plan for mental health treatment of children, failed. A federal judge may order an end to one program, but cannot order legislation to replace one policy with another.

Second, high start-up costs were advanced by deLeon as an obstacle to termination. Ironically, the cost of ending the training schools and funding psychiatric care, or of incurring start-up costs and building community-based group homes, was the same; the only choice was whether to pay now or pay later, and Oklahoma decided to pay later, on the back end. Given that no effective alternative to the closed training schools was formulated by the legislature, the judiciary accessed the state's Medicaid funds through the INT adjudication procedure. "Reallocation of . . . money from the psychological services to prevention efforts would cut . . . costs considerably," explained Claudette

Selph, executive director of the Parent-Child Center of Tulsa.[23] She continued, "We're paying for it now—we're just paying for it on the back end."

Third, another obstacle identified by deLeon is the dynamic system of public policies, ever responding to and changing with their environment. The state training schools defined the policy of the juvenile justice system: maintain a secure detention facility for dependent children who need long-term care and for whom foster parents cannot be found. Once the schools were ordered closed, psychiatric hospitals (another variation of a secure detention facility) were an easy organizational substitute, especially when funding could be obtained through Medicaid, without the vote of the legislature. The policy of institutionalization searched for another organization once the training schools were shut down.

Fourth, Kaufman's organizational threshold test also helps to understand the Oklahoma experience. The medium of the state training schools would score high on Kaufman's thickness indicators. Training schools are highly labor intensive; that is, the product is human service delivery to a captive population of dependent children. Training school personnel are usually highly educated—special education teachers, certified counselors, child care workers, psychologists, psychiatrists, administrative staff—all linked together through professional training offered by the state's several universities. The personnel of the training schools are paralleled within the state's many school districts and psychiatric hospitals, and combined contribute to a high energy consumption: there is much employment activity in this field. As a medium, training schools score high on almost all of Kaufman's organizational thickness indicators.

The treatment of emotionally troubled children, be it by training schools, school districts, or psychiatric hospitals, is a crowded, dense environment that has given rise to complex organizations. Given the thickness of this organizational medium, it is not surprising that while a court order could terminate a particular program variation, that is, training schools, it could not terminate the medium within which these schools existed. The medium only strengthened the institution-based programs, which remained operating after the training schools closed down. The personnel, the careers, the professions, and the degree and training programs connected with the training schools shifted over to the school districts and the psychiatric hospitals. Organizations may come and go, but careers, professions, and an organization's medium last one or more human lifetimes.

Earlier, deLeon explained that institutional permanence and anti-termination coalitions are obstacles to termination. Perhaps an organization's medium, and the medium's thickness, may itself possess a permanence that maintains a life of its own, beyond the realm of the termination of organizations and programs connected to it. Perhaps an organization's medium, if thick enough, is itself a type of antitermination coalition.

Fifth, deLeon has also observed that fundamental questions of values and ideologies, rather than economies and efficiencies, provide the grounds for termination. The Oklahoma training schools were closed as part of a nationwide deinstitutionalization movement and not as a result of economic analysis. The same changing ideology behind the deinstitutionalization of California's mental health system was also behind deinstitutionalizing the Oklahoma juvenile justice system. Why did Oklahoma rely on psychiatric hospitalization when it is the most costly and least effective intervention for treating emotionally disturbed children? Because efficiency and effectiveness had nothing to do with the decision to terminate the training schools; closing the schools was consistent with the ideology of deinstitutionalization. As Cameron reported in the case of California, termination occurred despite the lack of clinical or economic justification. Values and ideologies, not economies and efficiencies, were behind the decision to terminate the training schools.

In sum, the termination of the training schools was accompanied by the continuation of the policy of institutionalization due to five reasons: first, the intellectual reluctance of legislators to develop a parallel replacement policy; second, the misperceived high start-up costs of alternative programs, which were in reality the same cost of funding psychiatric care through Medicaid; third, the policy of detention was part of a dynamic system that searched, and found, an alternative organization in psychiatric hospitals; fourth, the medium within which institutionalized programs for the treatment of dependent children operated possessed an organizational thickness that was itself an obstacle to termination; and, fifth, because the initial decision to terminate the schools was based upon the ideology of deinsitutionalization, rather than on economic analysis, there were no cost considerations to guide future decisions about treatment alternatives.

Conclusion

The case of the Oklahoma Public Training Schools provides additional supporting evidence of the usefulness of deLeon's termination model. Similar to Frantz's research on the National Leprosarium presented in chapter 2, deLeon's model provides an explanation for the obstacles that prevented the deinstitutionalization of dependent children. Kaufman's threshold test explains the failure of termination in the light of the thick organizational medium in which the training schools operated. In addition, deLeon's observation about the political and ideological nature of termination decision making helps to explain the absence of cost considerations for alternative treatment programs.

The challenge facing policy researchers is to conduct additional studies on policy and organization termination and to search for patterns in these termination experiences. Testing frameworks and identifying patterns will eventually enable researchers to make generalizations about and develop models for policy termination.

Whatever happened to Terry D.? "Everyone asks me where he is now," explained Steve Nozick, his attorney.[24] "I don't know. Several years after he became an adult, he was charged as an adult and spent time at McAlester" (a state prison). "Predictably, he grew up as an emotionally disturbed kid. Abused kids commit crimes. It's tragic, but it happens to hundreds of kids," he concluded.

The challenge facing the Oklahoma legislature, the officials at DHS, and the U.S. District Court is how many more hundreds of children will lead tragic lives in the absence of a coherent and comprehensive deinstitutionalized juvenile system. In Oklahoma's case, organizational termination ended with both a bang and a whimper. The program of training schools ended with an abrupt bang, but the policy of institutionalizing dependent children, now manifested by psychiatric hospitalization and detention, continues with a long whimper.

5

Implementing Policy Termination

This chapter examines the case of a successful policy termination: terminating the Medicaid program in Tennessee and replacing it with a new managed health care reform program. Frustrated by yearly revisions of Medicaid, and faced with over 1.5 million citizens with no medical coverage, Tennessee lawmakers decided to create a new health care system that would provide medical insurance for virtually every Tennessean: TennCare. Financed primarily with federal funds, TennCare delivers health services through managed care organizations (MCOs) such as Health Maintenance Organizations (HMOs) and Preferred Provider Organizations (PPOs). All Medicaid eligible and uninsured citizens are eligible for TennCare, and some participants share the costs of the program through premiums, deductibles, and co-payments, depending upon their ability to pay.

Because implementation of TennCare depended upon the successful termination of Medicaid, the case of TennCare provides an opportunity to explore the linkages between policy termination and policy implementation. This chapter reviews the steps that have been taken to terminate Medicaid and facilitate the implementation of TennCare. The chapter discusses the case of TennCare within the framework of Robert Behn's "Dozen Hints for the Would-be Terminator."[1] And the chapter attempts to identify what steps have been taken to ensure the successful implementation of TennCare.

Implementing Policy Termination: TennCare

During the five-year period from 1987 to 1992, Medicaid costs in Tennessee increased 500 percent, from $500 million to $2.5 billion. This increase was due, in part, to the reasons associated with the overall rising cost of health care; for example, the use of expensive sophisticated technology; innovative but costly treatment of illnesses such as heart disease; the increasing incidence of AIDS and cancer; the increasing number and longevity of the elderly population, who have a great need for health care; and the treatment of illnesses and injuries caused by alcohol and drug abuse.[2] In addition, the increase was a result of the spiraling numbers of individuals eligible for Medicaid, general inflation, and the increased pricing of health services. During the same five-year period, a report issued by the Tennessee Department of Finance and Administration (DFA) estimated that the number of Medicaid eligibles increased over 70 percent, from 507,934 to 878,981 individuals.[3]

Moreover, the current system of health care in the United States leaves approximately 40 million individuals uninsured as of 1994.[4] About 80 percent of the uninsured are employed, low-wage earners, often referred to as the "working poor" and their dependents.[5] Because uninsured individuals are usually unable to pay for health care services, they are less likely than their insured counterparts to obtain medical care, use preventive services, or receive adequate prenatal care.[6] Much of the 12 percent of fees that hospitals and physicians are unable to collect every year is a direct result of treating uninsured patients, and this revenue loss is shifted to insured patients through inflated billing procedures.[7] This so-called charity care (health care accountants call it "receivable write-offs") is passed on and increases the overall cost of health care to insured patients. The accounts receivable dilemma that results from treating uninsured patients leads some hospitals and physicians to deny admission to patients or to transfer patients to other health care facilities (known as "patient dumping").

Tennessee's DFA estimated that Medicaid's five-year trend from 1987 to 1992 would result in a 220 percent increase in cost by 1997, or approximately $5.5 billion. Based on the assumption that the federal share of Medicaid would remain constant, this $3 billion increase would be met by a $851 million tax increase, and health care benefit cuts of $2.6 billion. The most significant consequences of such massive benefit cuts would be the loss of coverage for thousands of Medicaid recipients, reductions in the rates of reimbursement for providers of health services, and additional cost shifts to insured patients.

But while Medicaid costs were spiraling, the cost of providing health care for Tennessee's 250,000 public employees actually declined by 1.2 percent. Governor Ned McWherter and Finance Commissioner David Manning attribute this cost containment to the system of health care available for state employees since 1988: managed care. Tennessee's state employees receive managed care through Blue Cross/Blue Shield of Tennessee, Inc., and have a choice of managed care indemnity, PPO, and HMO programs.

There are two principal types of managed care.[8] The first is the popular alternative to traditional "unmanaged" indemnity. Managed indemnity provides fee-for-service health service payments and utilizes regulatory-type controls to secure provider compliance with medical management standards. This typically takes the form of a preadmission certification requirement for hospitalization and a similar requirement of insurer authorization for length of hospital stay. Such review requirements are typically administered at a distance using "800" number access for reviewers unfamiliar with the local practice environment. Managed indemnity is often accompanied by a Preferred Provider Organization (PPO), which is a network of health care providers established to provide negotiated, discount rates for services. In return, participating providers obtain a large network of patient referrals.

The second type of managed care is the Health Maintenance Organization (HMO), which regulates health services for participants and receives a capitated rate for each participant regardless of service level. The per person rate is established based on actuarial data of the participating group of individuals. Some HMOs own their facilities and employ their physicians, and others contract for services with one or more groups of providers.

In June 1993, Governor McWherter announced his solution for the Medicaid crisis: the termination of Medicaid and the creation of TennCare, a managed care program that would cover virtually every uninsured Tennessean. In order to use Medicaid funding for the new TennCare plan, McWherter would have to apply for a Section 1115 Demonstration Waiver for review and approval by Donna E. Shalala, secretary of the U.S. Department of Health and Human Services, and Health Care Financing Administration (HCFA). The waiver would be good for one year and would require reapproval.

The termination of Medicaid is an example of what deLeon earlier referred to as program termination. Although the program of Medicaid was eliminated, the general strategy of the State of Tennessee offering health services to the poor was retained and even expanded. Also, the organization that delivered Medicaid, the Department of Medicaid, Department of Health Services, was not terminated but was used to operate the TennCare program.

At least in theory, TennCare incorporated many aspects of health care reform that are currently discussed on a national level. Among these are the following:[9]

1. *Global budgeting:* Medicaid was a fee-for-service program, and the budget was essentially the amount billed by health care providers. Unlike Medicaid, TennCare uses cost containment and competitive marketplace contracting as part of the budget process.
2. *A standard benefit package:* all health care providers who wish to contract for managed care services must offer the same benchmark coverage.
3. *Pooling of purchasing power:* Because of the cost containment features of managed care, TennCare's projected savings are used to extend coverage to 500,000 uninsured Tennesseans, including the working poor. In addition, all health care providers who wish to treat the 250,000 state employees under the Blue Cross/Blue Shield program must also contract for TennCare patients. The combined purchasing power of these groups of potential patients (approximately 1.75 million people) provides lower-cost pricing of health care services.
4. *Managed care:* Through a "gatekeeper" approach, TennCare combines the allocation of resources for patients with professional judgment about the needs of patients.
5. *Incentives for preventive care:* Unlike Medicaid, TennCare provides preventive care at low or no cost. This feature will keep TennCare's pool of people healthier and assist in earlier diagnosis of serious illness, both of which help control health care costs.

6. *Elimination of welfare incentives:* Medicaid eligibility is compli-
    cated and often results in some members of a family eligible
    and others not. While not all individuals on public assistance
    are eligible for Medicaid, all Medicaid patients receive public
    assistance. Leaving the public assistance roll to accept a low-in-
    come job means losing Medicaid and, for all practical purposes,
    losing medical care access. Unlike Medicaid, TennCare covers
    all uninsured people.
7. *Cost sharing:* TennCare is available at no cost for individuals
    with income below an established "poverty level." For those
    above the poverty level, there is a sliding deductible, co-pay-
    ment, and monthly premium, based on percentile above the pov-
    erty level.
8. *Quality control:* Compared to Medicaid, TennCare provides
    greater monitoring and oversight.
9. *Elimination of class distinctions:* In the past, some health care
    providers refused to treat Medicaid patients, and patients receiv-
    ing treatment from some participating providers complained of
    receiving poorer services than private-pay patients. By combin-
    ing former Medicaid patients with all uninsured individuals, and
    by requiring that providers who contract to treat state employ-
    ees must also treat TennCare patients, the stigma of being a
    Medicaid patient was intended to be removed. Nonetheless,
    many physicians refuse to see TennCare patients during regular
    office hours and instead maintain separate "TennCare patient"
    appointments.

In their original study of implementation, Pressman and Wildavsky
emphasized that the formation and approval of a policy or program
does not necessarily mean that it will be carried out, become operational, or be implemented.[10] For example, the formation and approval
of TennCare was not the same as carrying out health care reform: the
implementation of TennCare depended upon the termination of the
Medicaid program. Only after Medicaid was terminated could Tenn-
Care become operational.

In order to explore the linkages between policy termination and
policy implementation and evaluate the usefulness of a termination
framework, Robert Behn's twelve guidelines for successful termination will be applied to the case of TennCare.

Testing Behn's Twelve Termination Guidelines

Hint One: Don't Float Trial Balloons

The so-called trial balloon is an intelligent political tactic that tests support and opposition among the legislature and the public for particular policy initiatives. Depending upon the initial reactions toward a policy, proposals can be revised or even quietly dropped. Nonetheless, Behn points out that a termination trial balloon does not produce positive results. Those who have a vested interest in the policy quickly mobilize opposition to block the termination.

One distinctive aspect of the termination of Medicaid in Tennessee is that no trial balloons were launched. On June 16, 1993, Governor McWherter and DFA Commissioner Manning released the application for the Medicaid waiver with a start-up date of January 1, 1994. Within just six months, McWherter had to obtain the waiver from HCFA; negotiate managed care contracts with MCOs; inform all eligible citizens about the new program; enroll participants and obtain their initial MCO choices; and orient health care providers about the administrative and financial changes brought about by TennCare. The reason for such speed was the anticipated opposition from the state's greatest organized special interest group: the Tennessee Medical Association (TMA).

The TMA felt that TennCare's reimbursement rates would be inadequate because of below-cost fee schedules and "overzealous MCO withholding."[11] Mark Greene, executive director of the TMA, cynically observed that "the governor couldn't afford 1 million people on Medicaid, so he handed it over to providers through TennCare and now 1.5 million people will be covered with the same revenue."[12] The state contacted Medicaid recipients in October 1993, informed them about the proposed changes, and requested that they return an enclosed ballot to state Medicaid officials by November 1 and identify which new provider they had selected. This "ballot" resulted in a deluge of calls to physicians by patients asking for advice about enrollment. According to Mark Greene, "in some places the volume of calls to physicians' offices has just about ground business to a halt."[13]

One doctor wrote a sarcastic (but very humorous) letter to the governor, who owns a trucking company, and suggested the governor try hauling "large quantities of material at 25 percent to 50 percent of your usual charges, even though these may not at times be equal to your cost."[14]

TMA asked its 6,700 members to contribute $200 each toward the cost of a lawsuit against the state, for a total of $1,340,000. The filing of the lawsuit was planned for January 1, 1994, the same date as the start-up of TennCare. The TMA claimed that TennCare was unconstitutional because it gave too much administrative power to the executive branch of government and took power away from the legislature, which is the appropriate branch of government to initiate health care reform. TMA also claimed that the governor was behind TennCare's "secret development," which "provided no advance notice or opportunity to comment on the proposed rules governing TennCare," and which TMA therefore felt violated the Tennessee Administrative Procedures Act.[15]

The officials at HCFA were not initially supportive of a waiver. An associate administrator of HCFA observed that 1,220 faxes were received in one week's time from Tennessee physicians and about 200 letters from Medicaid recipients opposing the waiver.[16] HCFA also questioned $595 million claimed by the governor's application as state-provided revenue that was actually the estimated amount of charity care traditionally offered by physicians and hospitals.[17] Governor McWherter blamed the delay on heavy lobbying by Tennessee doctors of HCFA officials in Washington.[18] The governor, a land mine engineer in the U.S. Army Reserves, dismissed the delay by saying, "We're in a mine field and we're laying bridges to get out."[19]

Governor McWherter responded by contacting fellow Democrat President Clinton about the prospects of bypassing HCFA's waiver procedures and receiving an executive order to have the waiver issued.[20] The TMA charged that bypassing HCFA would be unconstitutional and threatened a federal lawsuit if an executive order was issued.

Finally, Governor McWherter agreed to cut $300 million out of the estimated amount of charity care, lowered the number of covered participants from 1.8 million to 1.5 million with a cap of 1.3 million until June 30, 1994, and received the waiver from HCFA.[21] TennCare received approval only five months after requested, in large part because it was one step ahead of organized opposition. As Behn observes, "the case against termination is easy to make. The case for termination is much more difficult." He continues, "Terminators put themselves at a further disadvantage if they do not make a complete and detailed argument for termination before opponents can mobilize opposition." Governor McWherter's application for a HCFA waiver, a total of 137 pages in length, was a comprehensive and detailed case for the termination of Medicaid. The confidential formulation, coupled with the swiftness of the application, helped to limit the mobilization of opposition groups, in particular the TMA.

Hint 2: Enlarge the Policy's Constituency

Every public policy has its own constituency, a group of people who have a vested interest in its continuation and stable level of funding. Behn points out that unless those advocating termination are able to attract a new group of constituents, the policy's original clients will control debate and ensure continuation of the policy. TennCare's clientele was not only former Medicaid patients but also impoverished individuals who for some reason did not qualify for Medicaid, the working poor, and all other uninsured individuals. Ironically, a recent survey by the American Medical Association revealed that during 1992, about one-third of the nation's physicians did not offer health insurance to their employees.[22] Many of the uninsured who work for physicians will now be able to have insurance coverage. The enlarged clientele of TennCare provided a new constituency that supported the end of Medicaid. Governor McWherter tied the end of Medicaid to the expanded coverage of TennCare.

Hint 3: Focus Attention on the Policy's Harm

Behn suggests that the best way to attract constituents who will support termination is to focus attention on the harm caused by the policy. From the very beginning of Medicaid's proposed termination, the case was made by Governor McWherter and DFA Commissioner Manning that Medicaid was harmful. The DFA developed a slide presentation entitled *MEDICAID: Tennessee's Health Care Problem*.[23] The first slide is labeled "The Problem" and lists four problems: 1. unmanageable growth; 2. little flexibility; 3. fails the working poor; 4. encourages dependency on welfare. The next slides present graphs showing the spiraling trend of Medicaid costs and the increases needed from taxation and the massive cuts in services required to meet the increased costs. Finally included is a slide labeled "Only 3 Solutions

Exist": 1. raise taxes (every year); 2. massive health care reductions (every year); 3. fundamental change. Although the slide show went on to present the case for TennCare, the initial point of the presentation was that Medicaid was so harmful that only one solution existed: termination.

Hint 4: Take Advantage of Ideological Shifts to Demonstrate Harm

As a set of beliefs, ideology establishes the central premise for assessing all policy initiatives within the scope of the ideology. For example, Behn found that the ideology of "deinstitutionalization" undermined the legitimacy of incarcerating institutions. This ideology helped to pave the way for closing the Massachusetts Public Training Schools. The predominant ideology for health policy during the period of Tennessee's Medicaid waiver request was health care reform. President Clinton's Task Force on National Health Reform issued their report early in 1993, paving the ideological way for health care reform in Tennessee. The report emphasized the savings that would occur for all states, through the use of managed care health alliances, once the National Health Plan was operational. In Tennessee, the report's projected savings broke down to $1.1 billion for the state, $715 million for employers, and $899 million for workers by the year 2000.[24] The atmosphere of national health reform underscored the concept of reform for Tennessee. The notion that health reform was something that was about to happen, and that Tennessee would be leading the way for the other American states, further helped to bring about Medicaid's termination.

Hint 5: Inhibit Compromise

Even though termination advocates can demonstrate how a policy is harmful, not everyone will accept that harm has been proven, and still others will consider the harm a necessary cost of the policy's benefits. Proposed termination usually results in compromise between those who see the policy as harmful and needing to end and those who want the policy to continue. Compromise is one way policies and organizations can avoid termination and ensure their survival. Preventing compromise becomes a necessary action for successful termination.

The cost savings from the termination of Tennessee's Medicaid was dependent upon TennCare's managed care services operating in a way similar to the Blue Cross/Blue Shield of Tennessee (BCBS) plan offered for 1 million state employees. However, TennCare would pay less for certain services than BCBS. Why would providers contract with TennCare if they will subsequently receive comparatively lower payments for services? Governor McWherter had the answer: require all providers who want to contract with BCBS of Tennessee also to contract with TennCare. The TMA called this requirement "a big stick" to force doctors to join TennCare and accept lower payments for some of their patients.[25] In a letter to HCFA, TMA's general counsel wrote that "the phrase 'cram down' which physicians are using to describe the BCBS TennCare contract is appropriate since it so effectively symbolizes how the state is trying to enlist physician support."[26] The TMA encouraged all 8,000 Tennessee doctors to boycott BCBS of Tennessee, of which 7,000 were members, and most doctors announced plans to end their contract with BCBS of Tennessee on January 1, 1994, the start-up date for TennCare.

DFA Commissioner Manning responded by saying that the BCBS requirement allowed the state to use the leverage it has in the marketplace to "ensure the best price and access."[27] The TMA requested HCFA to increase the level of payments for certain treatments before granting a waiver. Governor McWherter threatened to recommend a renewal of an expiring tax on hospitals and to broaden it to cover doctors if payments under TennCare were increased.

McWherter did not compromise and instead used the BCBS contract as a "big stick" to obtain TennCare contracts with providers and threatened a tax on hospitals and doctors if the reimbursement rates were increased. Only days after HCFA granted the waiver, a senior vice-president of BCBS of Tennessee announced that doctors were coming back to the plan and renewing their contracts for the next year. Even Dr. Charles White, president of the TMA, finally agreed to sign contracts with MCOs to treat TennCare patients.[28]

Hint 6: Recruit an Outsider as Administrator/Terminator

Termination is a political struggle and as such needs a political leader to direct the termination efforts. The question is how often a prudent political leader would take on an assignment that is successful only if compromise is not allowed. Politics is compromise, and political leaders who want to win all-or-nothing struggles soon find themselves with numerous political enemies. Therefore, Behn reasons that an outsider who intends to leave the affected agency will be much more willing to voice potentially unpopular opinions and risk damaging his or her political future. For example, Behn's study of the Massachusetts Training Schools explained how Commissioner Jerome Miller was specifically hired to terminate the schools. He came from an academic position in Ohio and planned to stay only a few years, anticipating that he would make so many enemies that he would be forced to leave.

Governor McWherter did not bring in an outsider to terminate Medicaid. A well-told anecdote is that he and DFA Commissioner Manning were sitting next to one another on an airplane, and they developed the idea of TennCare on a napkin while writing on their food trays. The issue that surrounds the idea of an outside terminator is the ability to speak and act without regard to a future political career. McWherter was in his second term as governor and could not run for reelection in 1994. Governors realize, as do U.S. presidents, that there are certain policy initiatives that are best left for the second term of office: issues so controversial or potentially damaging that they are best left until reelection is not at stake.

While not an outsider, McWherter was in his next to last year as governor when the Medicaid waiver was requested. While realizing that he would make many political enemies during a struggle with the state medical association, he also realized that he would soon be leaving office.

Hint 7: Avoid Legislative Votes

Behn concludes that termination is more likely to result from executive than from legislative action. First, legislative leaders tend to have seniority, are on key committees, and are most likely connected to past decisions about the proposed policy to be terminated. They are the political leaders most likely to oppose, not propose, termination. Second, legislatures facilitate compromise, an activity not associated with termination. Informal approval from key legislative leaders, Behn concludes, is the best way to obtain legislative support.

TennCare was from the start a policy initiative of the executive branch of government. McWherter received legislative permission to apply for a Medicaid waiver; however, the content of the TennCare plan was developed by officials in the Department of Health and the Department of Finance and Administration. TMA was correct in its allegation that hearings and notices of Medicaid changes were not given and that the TMA was kept out of the reform efforts made by state administrators.

Past research has shown that state medical associations are usually consulted by legislative committees about changes in medical practice regulations.[29] One of the main responsibilities of the executive director of a state medical association is to prepare and deliver presentations and testimony before legislative committees. This results in substantial influence over all medical practice rules and legislation by state medical associations. Sometimes, a state medical association is requested to provide draft legislation, in which case the medical association is actually regulating the practice of its members. Keeping the development of TennCare within the executive branch of government kept the TMA out of health reform efforts and denied the TMA the opportunity for compromise.

Hint 8: Do Not Encroach Upon Legislative Prerogatives

Months after the January 1 starting date of TennCare, more than two dozen bills were still pending in the legislature to change certain parts of the program. Some of the bills were intended to weaken the "cram down" provision that requires providers for the state employees' BCBS plan also to accept TennCare patients. Others dealt with fears MCOs would shortchange the needs of the seriously mentally ill now that TennCare would be delivering mental health services to patients served previously by the state through Medicaid.

Behn observes that terminators who usurp the prerogative of the legislative branch, or even appear to do so, run the risk of turning potential supporters into opponents. Acknowledging the legal right of legislators to change the TennCare program, McWherter "begged" them to defeat the pending bills. He explained, "I'm not opposed to them, I just don't want them to pass. The members of the legislature brought those bills because they're concerned and I respect them."[30] Recognizing that there were problems to be solved, McWherter urged legislators to give his office a chance to improve the administration of the program without resorting to legislation.

The last legislation to be defeated was the "anti–cram down" bill; it died quietly in subcommittee. The sponsor of the bill lamented the legislature's unwillingness to address constituents' problems with legislation.[31] Governor McWherter responded to opposition legislation by correcting the glitches in TennCare addressed by the bills and not by opposing the legislation itself. By avoiding a heavy-handed approach to opposition bills, McWherter also avoided any appearance of encroaching upon legislative prerogatives.

Hint 9: Accept Short-term Cost Increases

"I think they should have left Medicaid alone. All this was jumped into before they thought it through," said Debbie Armstrong, mother of a blind twenty-year-old in a wheelchair with the mental functioning of a toddler.[32] She had just found out that the pediatrician who was familiar with her son's medical history was not an authorized TennCare provider, and that she must now search for a new doctor.

Terminating public policy sometimes costs more in the short run than continuing it. For example, while Massachusetts was closing its training schools and replacing them with group homes, it continued payroll for both groups of employees in order to avoid opposition by training school workers. Termination may result in a short-term rise in costs in order to achieve long-term savings. One cost of TennCare's rapid implementation—it started just eight months after the governor unveiled his creation—was that there were numerous operational problems resulting from such an early start-up date.

Confusion reigned at local emergency rooms as patients arrived unsure of what MCO plan they were in and hospitals tried to learn if their services were covered under TennCare.[33] State officials investigated the death of a baby whose mother says she was denied health care by area hospitals.[34] The mother claimed that hospital emergency rooms would not see her and that she was unable to get an appointment at clinics that contract with TennCare. Former Medicaid patients are accustomed to receiving care through emergency rooms, but TennCare limits payment for emergency room treatment of anything less than critical illness or trauma-type injuries.

TennCare also affected specialties such as dental and vision services. Without Medicaid's level of reimbursement, some high-volume vision operations went out of business and left patients to search for optometrists who participated in TennCare.[35] Jim Moss, president of Jackson–Madison County General Hospital repeated his call for the implementation of TennCare to be slowed.[36] The rapid implementation of TennCare was necessary to keep one step ahead of opposition groups, and to inhibit compromise. But its intended long-term savings resulted in programmatic and, in some cases, human short-term costs.

Hint 10: Buy Off the Beneficiaries

Short-term costs may be a result of coopting interest groups opposed to termination. Behn suggests that government employees who administer the policy are easiest to buy off: they can be offered new jobs. McWherter bought off the state Medicaid employees by assuring them that none would lose their jobs as a result of TennCare.

Another example of buying off the beneficiaries is the elimination of the Hospital Services Tax. The original TennCare plan included the elimination of this gross receipts–based tax, which brought in over $202 million yearly. This tax reduction was an inducement to the hospitals across the state, which form a major health finance interest group. Once opposition to the plan began, McWherter threatened to reimpose the tax and expand it to include physicians' practices. Eliminating this tax from TennCare served two purposes: it was a buy off of potential opposition groups, and it served to undermine opposition when McWherter threatened to reimpose and expand the tax.

Hint 11: Advocate Adoption, Not Termination

Political leaders prefer to initiate new and improved policies rather than end existing policies. The logic to employ, according to Behn, is that "the termination of Policy A may be best realized through the adoption of Policy B, when the selection of B necessitates the elimination of A."

McWherter talked more about the approval of TennCare than he did about the termination of Medicaid. Most of TennCare is an MCO type of Medicaid, and the majority of revenue that funds TennCare is supplied by the federal government and would be spent through a Medicaid program if TennCare did not exist. If McWherter had focused attention on the termination of Medicaid, TennCare's opposition would have had an easier target. By focusing on health care reform and the beginning of a new program, McWherter forced his opponents to argue against a new health care reform program, instead of arguing against the elimination of the established program of Medicaid.

This results in a certain amount of confusion: is the implementation of TennCare the beginning of a new program or the termination of an old program? In this case, implementing the termination of Medicaid means the beginning of TennCare.

Hint 12: Terminate Only What Is Necessary

The motivation of terminators should be to indicate precisely which aspects of a policy must end and which can continue. The less terminated, the smaller the number of people threatened by the termination, and the lower the amount of opposition. TennCare involved the termination of the fee-for-service program of Medicaid, but the policy of government-funded health services for impoverished individuals continued. TennCare did not terminate any of the services previously supplied by Medicaid, although the delivery of those services underwent change. The method of payment underlying the Medicaid system was terminated, but the health services components were retained in a different form.

Conclusion

This chapter has tested the termination implementation framework of Robert Behn and found it to provide an accurate explanation for the successful termination of Medicaid in Tennessee. Behn modestly warned his readers that his dozen hints for policy terminators were not a final guide to planning termination; he pointed out that they were not "Ironclad Laws That Guarantee Termination." Nonetheless, the program termination of Medicaid through the implementation of TennCare seems to have used Behn's hints as a blueprint. Behn's framework for implementing policy termination may not be "ironclad laws," but they are more than just hints. The case of TennCare has demonstrated that Behn's framework is not only useful for explaining policy termination but could also be applicable for planning termination.

6

Evaluating Termination Research

Peter deLeon has listed three tasks that face policy termination researchers.[1] First, case studies of policy termination should be compiled. Second, analysts should use these case studies to acquire an understanding of the factors leading to termination and build theories of policy termination. And third, the first two tasks can lead to strategies and tactics to promote termination.

This book has conducted a comprehensive analysis of policy and organization terminations in order to determine why they are terminated, how they are terminated, and what often prevents them from being terminated. Consistent with deLeon's three tasks, the case studies of termination presented in this book were compiled in order to draw generalizations about the factors associated with the process of termination. The overall goal has been to identify theories of termination that have been supported by research and strategies and tactics that are conducive to successful termination. Based on the research reviewed and presented so far, what conclusions can be made about policy and organization termination?

Conclusions from Termination Research

Seven generalizations can be made about policy and organization termination: (1) termination rarely has economic justification; (2) termi-

Table 6.1

Seven Conclusions About Policy and Organization Termination

1. Termination rarely has economic justification.
2. Termination is highly political and hard to achieve.
3. Termination requires cooptation of opponents.
4. Termination often involves changing ideologies.
5. Termination is followed by rebirth.
6. Successful termination is difficult to predict.
7. Termination is an American political paradox: everyone supports it, everyone opposes it.

nation is highly political and hard to achieve; (3) termination requires the cooptation of opponents; (4) termination often involves changing ideologies; (5) termination is often followed by rebirth; (6) successful termination is difficult to predict; (7) termination is an American political paradox: everyone supports it, everyone opposes it (see Table 6.1). These seven conclusions are discussed below.

1. Termination Rarely Has Economic Justification

Termination can rarely be justified in economic terms. Termination usually costs more than policy continuation, at least in the short run. Peter deLeon has observed that termination is usually the result of political rather than analytical decision making.[2] Political values and ideologies, according to deLeon, often pave the way for termination, instead of economies or efficiencies.

For example, Sunset legislation resulted in the termination of hundreds of state organizations and programs and realized substantial cost savings for many state governments. As explained in chapter 3, however, saving money was not the driving force behind the adoption of Sunset legislation. Instead, Sunset was driven by the political objectives of weak state legislatures to strengthen their oversight activities and obtain greater power over the governor and the administrative apparatus of state government.

Janet Frantz analyzed the attempted termination of the hospitals of the Public Health Service and concluded that cost savings was not a reason supporting termination and that short-term cost increases may be an unintended result of termination.[3]

The case of the Oklahoma Public Training Schools, presented in chapter 4, also underscores the relative unimportance of cost factors in termination. Once the federal court closed the schools, Oklahoma relied upon the most costly and least effective method for treating emotionally disturbed youth: institutionalization in psychiatric hospitals paid for through the state-administered Medicaid budget. Oklahoma spent each year in Medicaid funds an amount equal to that needed to build statewide decentralized, deinstitutionalized, community-based programs. Economies or efficiencies had nothing to do either with Oklahoma's decision to close the schools or with the policy of institutionalization through hospitalization.

Even when cutting costs is behind a termination effort, it is not in itself a good enough reason to implement termination successfully. The main objective of the termination of Tennessee's Medicaid program, presented in chapter 5, was drastically to cut and stabilize Medicaid spending. But, it took far more than a cost-cutting argument for Tennessee's Governor McWherter to implement termination. The governor relied upon his strong leadership and his political skills in bullying and coopting potential opponents.

There is general agreement among researchers that while cost-cutting rhetoric may be used as a tactic by terminators, in reality no short-term savings result from termination.

2. Termination Is Highly Political and Hard to Achieve

The U.S. Air Force currently maintains a fleet of B-1 bombers despite efforts over a seven-year period to kill the project. The B-1 demonstrates the inherently political nature of termination: interest groups affected by a termination can almost always organize enough political resources to block the end of a program beneficial to the group. As a result of the death of the B-1, subcontractors in almost every congressional district would face a loss of revenue. Even after military leaders in the air force became skeptical of the importance of the production of the B-1, in the face of technical advances in airframe design and adjustments in defense strategy as a result of a changing geopolitical world,

Congress insisted on continued funding of B-1 production. Members of Congress wanted the flow of funds to continue to their districts, and air force brass scrambled to find a suitable role for the B-1. Apparently dead after the 1976 presidential election, the development of the B-1 continued with a whimper until the election of President Reagan in 1980. The B-1 was then raised from the dead and produced at a far greater cost than ever expected, resulting in the small fleet of B-1s in existence today.

Nowhere can the politics of termination be better seen than in the resourcefulness of affected groups opposed to termination. Opponents to termination have multiple access points within the political system to block termination, as confirmed by a number of scholars. Mitchel Wallerstein demonstrated how hard it was to cut or even limit veterans' disability benefits during the depression.[4] In the face of a well-organized opposition, "sacred cow" programs such as veterans' benefits or Social Security have little chance to be cut or terminated. Abram N. Shulsky related the unsuccessful efforts to terminate the Washington, DC, police motorcycle squad,[5] which involved pressure from opponents not only through the municipal political system but also through the congressional subcommittee that provides oversight for the district. Both these cases underscore the strength that anti-termination coalitions have in preventing terminations.

Peter deLeon has identified antitermination coalitions as one of the main obstacles to termination.[6] Building on deLeon's work, Janet Frantz found antitermination coalitions were behind the unsuccessful attempt to terminate the National Leprosarium Hospital.[7] Michael Harris concluded that antitermination coalitions were behind the failure of the Israeli government to terminate the failing kibbutzim.[8] Even though some kibbutzim will never be financially self-sufficient, the organized opposition by the Labor party was a successful obstacle to termination. Finally, chapter 4 presented the termination of Oklahoma's Public Training Schools, where once again antitermination coalitions were successful in retaining the policy of institutionalizing emotionally disturbed children.

The American political system is characterized by multiple access points to government. Affected interest groups can gain access to government decision-making processes through legislative hearings, the enactment of legislative bills, the executive branch, the bureaucratic apparatus of government, the courts, and even through the media.

These multiple points of access provide many opportunities for organized groups to oppose changes in specific government programs. Thus, American politics usually results in small or incremental changes in public policy.

Opposition to termination can therefore come from multiple sources through multiple access points. Any attempt to terminate a government program, policy, or organization is potentially at the mercy of the entire political system. The reason termination is so difficult to achieve is because it is essentially political in nature. Termination is hard to accomplish within an incrementally oriented political system.

3. Termination Requires Cooptation of Opponents

Robert Behn's research demonstrates that termination is possible only through determined, prompt action by strong political administrators who are willing to engage, if necessary, in political cooptation of opponents.[9] In the case of the termination of the Massachusetts Public Training Schools, Behn relates how the primary terminator, Commissioner Miller, sidestepped the common survival tactics practiced by targeted agencies. Miller practiced textbook cooptation: he avoided the opposition of school employees by continuing to keep them on the payroll even though the schools were closed; he avoided the need for legislative support and kept the issue of termination out of legislative review; he engaged the support of the governor's spouse; he obtained public support by portraying the abuses of the schools; and he compromised by dropping his efforts to retrain the staff and satisfied himself with just closing the schools.

Behn's experience with the Massachusetts experience led him to develop his set of "hints" for implementing termination.[10] Taken as a theoretical framework, these dozen hints were applied in chapter 5 to explain the successful termination of Tennessee's Medicaid program. In this case, Tennessee's Governor McWherter practiced the politics of cooptation in his efforts to terminate the old Medicaid program and replace it with a lower-cost, managed care program designed by his chief aide, the commissioner of the Department of Finance and Administration. McWherter moved fast to avoid opposition from the Tennessee Medical Association, avoided legislative votes, enlarged the clientele served by the state health program, threatened the hospital industry with additional taxes, and constantly emphasized the harm that the old Medicaid program was inflicting on the state's budget. It was almost as though McWherter used Behn's dozen hints for termination as a blueprint for his own successful termination of Medicaid; within a period of about three months, Medicaid was dead and TennCare, the new health program, was in place.

In both the Massachusetts and Tennessee cases, political leaders of termination successfully blocked or cut off the political access points of opposition groups. The politics of cooptation is an important ingredient for successful termination.

4. Termination Often Involves Changing Ideologies

Successful termination is often the result of a change in the application of certain principles, or assumptions, about what services are appropriate for government to sponsor or how these services should be delivered. These principles can be political, social, or economic. James Cameron defines these guiding principles or assumptions as ideologies.[11] Because ideologies can be neither proved nor disproved, the application of ideology to the continued existence of a program does not involve issues of performance, effectiveness, cost, or economies. Instead, termination in this case is conducted on the basis of a change in principle.

Cameron explains how the ideology of deinstitutionalization in the treatment of mental illness resulted in the closing of state mental hospitals in California. The old ideology of institutionalizing the mentally ill gave way to the principle of community-based group homes. Patients were discharged from closed hospitals before local community health agencies were prepared to care for them with group homes. Some patients were transferred from one hospital to another, and others suffered from lack of shelter and proper medical care. The deinstitutionalization movement was also responsible for closing juvenile and children's mental health facilities, for example, the Massachusetts and Oklahoma Public Training Schools.

Ideology has also been behind other recent successful terminations. A change from liberal to conservative politics during the late 1970s and early 1980s led to the 1978 Airline Deregulation Act, which eliminated the Civil Aeronautics Board. The conservative politics of the Reagan administration also claimed the Department of Energy.

DeLeon's recent research has led him to conclude that questions of values and ideologies usually provide the grounds for termination.[12] DeLeon views policy termination as an exercise in political, as opposed to analytical, decision making. Although Eugene Bardach has described the advocates of termination as Oppositionists, Economizers, or Reformers,[13] rarely do the advocates fall into the category of Economizers. Instead, the ideological nature of termination corresponds to the categories of Oppositionists (those who want a policy terminated because they see it as flawed or bad) or Reformers (those who see termination as an opportunity to adopt new, better policies). DeLeon concludes that the "cost-benefit" types of analyses are rarely used to justify termination; instead, termination revolves around questions of who benefits and who loses and to what extent termination is consistent with changing political values.

In sum, changes in social, political, or economic ideology can offer political leaders a rare window for policy termination.

5. Termination Is Often Followed by Rebirth

After examining a variety of policy and organization termination experiences, termination appears to be a journey more than a destination. Agencies are resilient and often come back to life after the terminators have left the political scene. Those programs claimed by death face neither heaven nor hell, but a potential afterlife. There is life after death, at least in the public sector.

The work of Justin Greenwood,[14] Abram Shulsky,[15] and Mitchel Wallerstein[16] all confirm that terminated policies can be raised from the dead. Greenwood's examination of how terminated policies are manifested in successive policies suggests that terminated policies not only have an afterlife but are sometimes reincarnated. Greenwood finds that many terminations result in policy succession, or replacement, at a later date.

Shulsky related the experience of terminating the Washington, DC, police motorcycle squad. Even after the squad was disbanded, the motorcycles were seen during parade escorts and eventually found their way back on the streets. Wallerstein explored the difficulty of achieving and retaining budget cuts in entitlement benefits even during a depression when federal money was scarce.

The case of Oklahoma's Public Training Schools demonstrated that while a specific program may be terminated, the policy supporting that program can manifest itself through other programs in other bureaucratic locations. In this case, the schools were terminated, but the policy of institutionalizing emotionally disturbed children continued through state-contracted programs with psychiatric hospitals.

Terminated programs are not unlike the killer robot in the popular motion picture *Terminator II*: even when the robot is crushed and melted down to a liquid state, it reforms and comes back to life. Nothing can kill the terminator robot, nor can anyone eliminate the Washington, DC, police motorcycle squad.

6. Successful Termination Is Difficult to Predict

Several theoretical frameworks of termination have been repeatedly used by researchers in order to analyze termination experiences. The termination obstacles framework developed by deLeon[17] has been proven by both Frantz's[18] and Norris-Tirrell's[19] research to be very useful in explaining the termination experiences of different kinds of policies within different government settings. Kaufman's life-cycle theory of organizations has also received confirmation and support from several recent studies by Mueller,[20] Norris-Tirrell,[21] and Chackerian.[22] The case of Oklahoma's Public Training Schools presented in chapter 4 also provides support for both deLeon's and Kaufman's theories.

The termination framework of Robert D. Behn has also proved useful in explaining both the termination of the Massachusetts Public Training Schools and the termination of Tennessee's Medicaid program. As presented in chapter 5, Behn's "dozen hints" for implementing termination provided a blueprint for the successful termination of Tennessee's Medicaid program.

While the frameworks of deLeon, Kaufman, and Behn are useful in explaining termination experiences on an ex post facto basis, the predictive power of these frameworks is yet unproven. Only once a termination experience has concluded do these frameworks prove useful by providing a structure with which to analyze the case, whether or not the case has been successful. But the questions "Will this agency be terminated?" and "When will this agency be terminated?" have not so far been addressed by these frameworks.

For example, the timing of termination—that is, when an agency will actually die—is still something of a mystery. Samuel Best, Paul

Teske, and Michael Mintrom studied the death of the Interstate Commerce Commission and concluded that no termination theory can currently explain when an agency will be ended.[23] Kaufman's explanation that the timing of termination is left to chance, the luck of the draw, the randomness of the universe, is still as good as any explanation so far offered.

Alternatively, the meaning given or attributed to events over time may involve so subtle a process as to avoid detection by researchers. Perhaps something other than chance may be involved in the inability of researchers to pinpoint or predict the exact moment of termination. The interaction of social and economic events over time may create changes in an organization's environment beyond which the organization can respond effectively. If the organization cannot respond effectively and adequately to its changing environment, the organization becomes terminally ill and will soon die. If this interaction over time is so subtle as to escape the detection and measurement by researchers, however, then it may appear that no explanation can be given for the demise of the organization. Termination, in this case, only seems to rely on chance: what cannot be adequately measured or predicted is written off to chance or the benign randomness of the universe.

7. Termination Is an American Political Paradox: Everyone Supports It, Everyone Opposes It

The perception that government itself is a political problem facing this nation has been voiced by many recent politicians, including Ronald Reagan and Bill Clinton. Cutting government and making it smaller is a common theme found in political debates, especially during elections. As discussed in chapter 1, David Osborne and Ted Gaebler provide a textbook-type presentation of these political slogans in their book *Reinventing Government*.[24] These authors compare American government to fat people who need to lose weight, although they do not give the specific ingredients of their proposed diet. Nonetheless, the personnel reductions in the federal government that they call for would almost certainly involve terminating many government programs.

Before government can be reinvented, parts of it must be terminated and cast aside. This termination exercise must be accomplished within the boundaries of American government as it currently exists: a political system characterized by multiple access points for groups of individuals who oppose termination of specific programs that will adversely affect them.

From an administrative viewpoint, democracy is a messy political system that makes policy and organization termination an almost impossible task. For example, useless police motorcycle patrols cannot be eliminated in our nation's capital; the B-1 airplane, a bomber without a mission, was built at a cost of billions of dollars regardless of nationwide opposition; and, despite efforts at termination, the National Leprosarium continues to incarcerate victims of Hansen's disease needlessly. In each of these cases those groups affected by the termination of these programs lobbied effectively for program continuation.

President Clinton, in his 1996 State of the Union address to Congress, announced that the time had come for the end of government as we have come to know it. Simultaneously, he called for support from Congress for a number of new federal programs. Ultimately, public policy and organization termination is a political paradox: everyone is for it as long as it does not affect him or her personally, as long as no one is pinned down about which specific programs are to be terminated, and as long as plans for additional spending for new programs can be discussed at the same time.

The termination of public policies and organizations must take place within the context of an essential American political value: citizens have the right to voice their opinions about government and have their opinions represented by political leaders. The American political system also allows citizens the right to hold contradictory political viewpoints. For example, the vast majority of the American public simultaneously support a balanced federal budget and a cut in federal income taxes. American government is a pluralistic democracy in which multiple interest groups, representing different and conflicting public opinions, can take advantage of multiple access points into the political system. Opposition to terminating public programs, policies, and organizations is not only expected but is a political right of those adversely affected.

But this messy democracy also allows for the stability of government programs; politicians may come and go with each election year, but programs last one or more human lifetimes. Herbert Kaufman attributes the long life of government programs to the incremental decision making of American government.

It is no coincidence that in two of the successful terminations presented in this book—the termination of the Massachusetts Public Training Schools and the termination of Tennessee's Medicaid program—political leaders accomplished termination by sidestepping and bullying opposition groups and coopting other political opponents. Termination is easy when political leaders can limit democratic participation in public policymaking.

As mentioned in chapter 1, termination is an integral part of the American political process. As such, it must take place within the constraints of democratic values such as citizen participation, political representation, and old-time pork-barrel politics. Politicians will continue to call for cutting big government and ending certain programs, but few will identify which specific programs they have targeted. Those few political leaders who are serious about terminating policies or organizations will have to acknowledge the political realities of termination: successful terminations are the result of strong political leaders taking advantage of their knowledge of the political system by bullying, sidestepping, and coopting their political opponents. In a political system that emphasizes coalition building and compromise, those political leaders are few and far between, and will probably have a hard time getting reelected.

Termination will become an increasingly important issue as we begin the next century. As soon as baby boomers start to retire, the Ponzi-type financing of the Social Security system will require fundamental changes in benefits. Currently, retired beneficiaries are receiving more benefits than they have paid for. Benefits are funded by the current generation of working Americans through payroll deductions. But as the percentage of Americans receiving benefits increases, the ability of working Americans to pay for the benefits will be exhausted. Political leaders will increasingly turn to termination as a way of restructuring government programs.

The next century will also exacerbate the "scissors crisis," identified by Swedish political scientist Daniel Tarschys.[25] As Tarschys explains, the widening gap between receipts and outlays demands that governments all over the globe cut programs and restructure government. Increasing receipts is not the answer. So-called fiscal cannibalism, when one tax eats up the economic base of another tax, results in a critical level of taxation, beyond which additional taxes become self-defeating. Thus, the scissors effect: cut, cut, cut.

Conclusion

As mentioned previously, policy termination research has too often taken the form of a single case study, which is in some way idiosyncratic. Fifteen years ago, Robert Behn called for new thinking and research into policy termination: "The field of policy termination clearly needs a set of hypotheses with which to experiment and an expanded base of case studies—cases that explicitly address and attempt to test these hypotheses."[26]

Despite the research conducted since that time, the study of policy termination continues to be, in the words of Robert Biller, a "wrongly underattended issue."[27] Political leaders of the next century will find themselves facing tough termination decisions. Armed only with a pair of scissors, they may not be able to make the cuts necessary to support a healthy economy. Knowledge of termination through comparative research will provide insights into termination that will prove useful to political leaders facing tough political decisions involving cuts, rollbacks, and program terminations.

Twenty years ago, Eugene Bardach alleged that the leading cause for the lack of attention received by the study of policy termination was the lack of generalization offered by the few existing studies.[28] Single case studies, with little testing of theoretical frameworks, composed primarily of anecdotal data, do not attract the attention of social scientists.

One hopes that this book has provided a response to Bardach's charge. The case studies presented in the previous chapters were brought together in order to identify the theoretical frameworks of termination that have been supported by research. The seven conclusions about termination advanced in this chapter were a first attempt to generalize about how policies and organizations are terminated and what often prevents them from being terminated.

Academicians and other social scientists will pay increased attention to the study of policy termination with the repeated testing of the theoretical frameworks presented in this book. For now, the testing of policy termination theories falls short of what is needed for the kind of generalization made by other fields of social science. One hopes that additional studies will encourage ever increasing numbers of policy researchers to transform the study of policy termination from a wrongly underattended issue to one that is well attended.

Notes

Preface

1. Eugene Bardach, ed., "Policy and Program Termination," *Policy Sciences* 7, no. 2 (June 1976), special issue.

2. Garry Brewer and Peter deLeon, *The Foundations of Policy Analysis* (Homewood, IL: Dorsey Press, 1983).

3. Kaufman, Herbert, *Are Government Organizations Immortal?* (Washington, DC: Brookings, 1976); and *Time, Chance and Organizations: Natural Selection in a Perilous Environment* (Chatham, NJ: Chatham House, 1987).

4. Mark R. Daniels, "Implementing Policy Termination Health Care Reform in Tennessee," *Policy Studies Review 14,* no. 3/4 (Autumn/Winter 1996): 353–374. "Organizational Termination and Policy Continuation: Closing the Oklahoma Public Training Schools," *Policy Sciences* 28, no. 2 (June 1995): 301–316; "Termination, Innovation and the American States: Testing Sunset Legislation," *American Review of Politics* 15 (Winter 1995): 507–518.

5. Mark R. Daniels, "Terminating Bureaucracy: Ending Public Programs, Policies and Organizations," in *Handbook of Bureaucracy*, ed. Ali Farazmand (New York: Marcel Dekker, 1994), pp. 446–466.

6. Mark R. Daniels, ed., "Public Policy and Organizational Termination," a special issue of the *International Journal of Public Administration* (forthcoming, 1997), including (idem) an Introduction, "Theories for the Termination of Public Policies, Programs, and Organizations."

Chapter 1

1. For a complete discussion of the termination of the B-1, see Nicholas Wade, "Death of the B-1: The Events Behind Carter's Decision," *Science* 197

(August 5, 1977): 536–539. The most comprehensive treatment of the B-1 is found in Nick Kotz, *Wild Blue Yonder: Money, Politics, and the B-1 Bomber* (Princeton: Princeton University Press, 1988).

2. This is the title of Herbert Kaufman's book: *Are Government Organizations Immortal?* (Washington, DC: Brookings, 1976).

3. This definition is found in one of the leading public policy textbooks, written by Garry Brewer and Peter deLeon, *The Foundations of Policy Analysis* (Homewood, IL: Dorsey Press, 1983).

4. The best presentation of cutback management is given by Charles H. Levine in two books: *Managing Fiscal Stress: The Crisis in the Public Sector* (Chatham, NJ: Chatham House, 1980); and *The Politics of Retrenchment* (Beverly Hills, CA: Sage, 1982).

5. Downsizing is often discussed in terms of privatizing and decentralizing government services, for example, chapters 3, 7, 9, 10 in David Osborne and Ted Gaebler's popular book, *Reinventing Government: How the Entrepreneurial Spirit is Transforming the Public Sector* (New York: Penguin, 1993).

6. Garry Brewer, "Termination: Hard Choices, Harder Questions," *Public Administration Review* 38 (1978): 338–344.

7. Brewer and deLeon, *Foundations of Policy Analysis*.

8. Charles O. Jones, *An Introduction to the Study of Public Policy* (Monterey, CA: Brooks Cole, 1984).

9. Brewer and deLeon, *Foundations of Policy Analysis*.

10. Peter deLeon, "Policy Evaluation and Program Termination," *Policy Studies Review* 2, no. 4 (1983): 631–647.

11. Robert D. Behn, "Closing the Massachusetts Public Training Schools," *Policy Sciences* 7, no. 2 (June 1976): 151–171. Mark R. Daniels, "Organizational Termination and Policy Continuation: Closing the Oklahoma Public Training Schools," *Policy Sciences* 28, no. 2 (June 1995): 301–316.

12. Behn, "Closing the Massachusetts Public Training Schools."

13. Peter deLeon, "Public Policy Termination: An End and a Beginning," *Policy Analysis* 4 (1978): 369–392.

14. Ibid.

15. Ibid.; Kaufman, *Are Government Organizations Immortal?*

16. deLeon, "Public Policy Termination."

17. Ibid.; Kaufman, *Are Government Organizations Immortal?*

18. deLeon, "Public Policy Termination."

19. Ibid.

20. Rep. Newt Gingrich, Rep. Dick Armey, and the House Republicans, *Contract with America* (New York: Random House, 1994).

21. Ibid., p. 23.

22. Ibid., p. 24.

23. Ibid., p. 23.

24. Osborne and Gaebler, *Reinventing Government*.

25. Vice-President Gore's book is based upon findings reported in the National Performance Review. Al Gore, *Creating a Government That Works Better and Costs Less* (New York: Penguin Books, 1993).

26. Osborne and Gaebler, *Reinventing Government*, p. 29.

27. Osborne and Gaebler also state that after the government has been restruc-

tured there should be a no-layoff policy. See *Reinventing Government*.

28. Peter deLeon, "Afterward: The Once and Future State of Policy Termination," *International Journal of Public Administration* 20 (1997).

29. Eugene Bardach, "Policy Termination as a Political Process," *Policy Sciences* 7, no. 2 (June 1976): 123–131.

30. Edward L. Katzenbach, "The Horse Calvary in the Twentieth Century: A Study of Policy Response," *Public Policy* 8 (1958): 120–149.

31. Bardach's symposium (including many of the articles cited here) appeared as a special issue of the journal *Policy Sciences* 7, no. 2 (June 1976): 123–243.

32. The textbook (*Foundations of Policy Analysis*) was written by Garry Brewer and Peter deLeon. The author of the two books is Herbert Kaufman: *Are Government Organizations Immortal?* (1976) and *Time, Chance and Organizations: Natural Selection in a Perilous Environment* (Chatham, NJ: Chatham House, 1987).

33. Peter deLeon, "Policy Termination as a Political Phenomenon," in *The Politics of Program Evaluation*, ed. Dennis Palumbo (Newbury Park, CA: Sage, 1987), pp. 173–199.

34. Robert P. Biller, "On Tolerating Policy and Organizational Termination: Some Design Considerations," *Policy Sciences* 7, no. 2 (June 1976): 133–149.

Chapter 2

1. Eugene Bardach, "Policy Termination as a Political Process," *Policy Sciences* 7, no. 2 (June 1976): 123–131.

2. *Policy Sciences* 7, no. 2 (June 1976): 123–243 (entire issue).

3. Bardach, "Policy Termination."

4. Bardach is referring to T.S. Eliot's poem "The Hollow Men" (1925), which more fully reads: "This is the way the world ends. Not with a bang but a whimper."

5. Robert P. Biller, "On Tolerating Policy and Organizational Termination: Some Design Considerations," *Policy Sciences* 7, no. 2 (June 1976): 133–149.

6. Robert D. Behn, "Closing the Massachusetts Public Training Schools," *Policy Sciences* 7, no. 2 (June 1976): 151–171.

7. This textbook is now considered a classic: Herbert A. Simon, Donald W. Smithburg, and Victor A. Thompson, *Public Administration* (New York: Knopf, 1950).

8. Ibid., p. 153.

9. Ibid., p. 157.

10. Ibid., p. 158.

11. Jeffrey L. Pressman and Aaron B. Wildavsky, *Implementation* (Berkeley: University of California Press, 1973), ch. 5.

12. Behn, "Closing the Massachusetts Public Training Schools," p. 160.

13. Ibid., p. 161.

14. Ibid., p. 162.

15. Robert D. Behn, "How to Terminate a Public Policy: A Dozen Hints for the Would-be Terminator," *Policy Analysis* 4, no. 3 (Summer 1978): 393–413.

16. Mitchel B. Wallerstein, "Terminating Entitlements: Veterans' Disability

Benefits in the Depression," *Policy Sciences* 7, no. 2 (June 1976): 173–182.

17. Abram N. Shulsky, "Abolishing the District of Columbia Motorcycle Squad," *Policy Sciences* 7, no. 2 (June 1976): 183–197. For a more recent treatment of terminating motorcycle squads, see Carol L. Ellis, "Program Termination: A Word to the Wise," *Public Administration Review* 43, no. 4 (1983): 352–357.

18. W. Henry Lambright and Harvey M. Sapolsky, "Terminating Federal Research and Development Programs," *Policy Sciences* 7, no. 2 (June 1976): 199–213.

19. Valerie J. Bradley, "Policy Termination in Mental Health: The Hidden Agenda," *Policy Sciences* 7, no. 2 (June 1976): 215–224.

20. James L. Foster and Garry D. Brewer, "And the Clocks Were Striking Thirteen: The Termination of War," *Policy Sciences* 7, no. 2 (June 1976): 225–243.

21. Herbert Kaufman, *Are Government Organizations Immortal?* (Washington, DC: Brookings, 1976); *Time, Chance, and Organizations: Natural Selection in a Perilous Environment* (Chatham, NJ: Chatham House, 1985).

22. Kaufman, *Time, Chance and Organizations*, p. 25.

23. Kaufman, *Are Government Organizations Immortal?* p. 55.

24. Kaufman, *Time, Chance and Organizations*, p. 27.

25. Ibid., p. 141.

26. Ibid., pp. 144–146.

27. Samuel M. Hines, "Organizations and Evolution: A Review of Herbert Kaufman's *Time, Chance and Organizations*," *Politics and the Life Sciences* 5 (1987): 266.

28. Elliot White, "A Review of *Time, Chance and Organizations*," *Politics and the Life Sciences* 5 (1987): 268.

29. Keith J. Mueller, "Federal Programs to Expire: The Case of Health Planning," *Public Administration Review* 48, no. 3 (May/June 1988): 719–725.

30. Richard Chackerian, "Reorganization of State Governments: 1900–1985," *Journal of Public Administration Research and Theory* 6, no. 1 (January 1996): 25–47. Although reorganization is not the same as termination, it provides an opportunity for testing Kaufman's theory of organizational development. As Chackerian points out, " . . . reorganization is a much less drastic change than a termination and therefore provides a conservative basis of comparison" (p. 43).

31. Peter deLeon, "Public Policy Termination: An End and a Beginning," *Policy Analysis* 4 (1978): 379–386; "A Theory of Policy Termination," in *The Policy Cycle*, ed. Judith V. May and Aaron B. Wildavsky (Beverly Hills, CA: Sage, 1978), pp. 286–292.

32. Janet E. Frantz, "Reviving and Revising a Termination Model," *Policy Sciences* 25 (1992): 175–189.

33. Peter deLeon, "Policy Termination as a Political Phenomenon," in *The Politics of Program Evaluation*, ed. Dennis Palumbo (Newbury Park, CA: Sage, 1987), pp. 173–199.

34. Ibid., p. 176.

35. James M. Cameron, "Ideology and Policy Termination: Restructuring California's Mental Health System," in May and Wildavsky, eds., *The Policy Cycle*, pp. 301–328.

36. Ibid., p. 306.

37. Ibid.

38. Ibid., p. 316.

39. deLeon, "Policy Termination as a Political Phenomenon," p. 191.

40. The symposium, entitled "Public Policy and Organization Termination," will be published in volume 20 of the *International Journal of Public Administration*.

41. Samuel Best, Paul Teske, and Michael Mintrom, "Terminating the Oldest Living Regulator: The Death of the Interstate Commerce Commission," *International Journal of Public Administration* 20, no. 12 (1997).

42. Janet E. Frantz, "The High Cost of Policy Termination," *International Journal of Public Administration* 20, no. 12 (1997).

43. Justin Greenwood, "The Succession of Policy Termination," *International Journal of Public Administration* 20, no. 12 (1997).

44. Michael Harris, "Policy Termination: Uncovering the Ideological Dimension," *International Journal of Public Administration* 20, no. 12 (1997).

45. Dorothy Norris-Tirrell, "Organization Termination in the Nonprofit Setting: The Dissolution of Children's Rehabilitation Services," *International Journal of Public Administration* 20, no. 12 (1997).

46. Peter deLeon, "Afterward: The Once and Future State of Policy Termination," *International Journal of Public Administration* 20, no. 12 (1997).

47. Ibid.

48. Ibid.

Chapter 3

1. Garry Brewer and Peter deLeon, *The Foundations of Policy Analysis* (Homewood, IL: Dorsey Press, 1978), p. 385.

2. Robert P. Biller, "On Tolerating Policy and Organizational Termination: Some Design Considerations," *Policy Sciences* 7, no. 2 (June 1976): 137.

3. Brewer and deLeon, *Foundations of Policy Analysis*, p. 187.

4. Robert D. Behn provides an excellent history of the attempts to enact Sunset legislation for the federal government in "The False Dawn of Sunset Laws," *Public Interest* 49 (Fall 1977): 103–118.

5. Ibid., p. 104.

6. Common Cause, *Status of Sunset in the States: A Common Cause Report* (Washington, DC: Common Cause, 1982), p. 3. This comprehensive report on the experience of state governments with Sunset was conducted by Common Cause, a Washington-based nonprofit reform group.

7. Ibid., p. 42.

8. The most recent survey of the states' experiences with Sunset is reported in an article by Richard C. Kearney: "Sunset: A Survey and Analysis of the State Experience," *Public Administration Review* 50 (January/February 1990): 49–57.

9. Common Cause, *Status of Sunset*, Appendix D; and ibid.

10. Common Cause, *Status of Sunset*, pp. 12–24.

11. Ibid., p. 53.

12. Kearney, "Sunset."

13. Ibid., p. 53.

14. Common Cause, *Status of Sunset*, p. 26.

15. Kearney, "Sunset," p. 55.

16. Virginia Gray, "Innovation in the States: A Diffusion Study," *American Political Science Review* 67 (1973): 1174–1185.

17. Jack L. Walker, "The Diffusion of Innovations among the American States," *American Political Science Review* 63 (1969): 880–899.

18. Ibid.

19. Gray, "Innovation in the States."

20. Robert L. Savage, "Policy Innovativeness as a Trait of American States," *Journal of Politics* 40 (1978): 212–224.

21. Given the relatively recent admission of Alaska and Hawaii into the federal union, it is not possible to score these two states on a variety of policies adopted during the last century or the early twentieth century.

22. Walker's rankings of states is based on the mean innovation scores of states on 88 policies, each one of which may be expressed as:

$$I = 1 - \frac{\overset{n}{\underset{I=1}{Y}}}{T}$$

where I = innovativeness score, Y = the number of years that have elapsed from the first adoption to a particular state's adoption, and T = the number of years elapsed for the diffusion of the policy to be complete. Savage's rankings are based on scores weighted for standard deviations, and Gray's rankings are the mean order of states adopting twelve policies.

23. Common Cause, *Status of Sunset*.

24. The statistic used on dichotomous dependent variables in this paper is the Mann-Whitney U. This is computed as the number of times a score from group 1 precedes a score from group 2, controlling for tied ranks. A nonrandom pattern is indicated by an extreme U. The area under the curve is computed by transforming U into the normally distributed Z. For further explanation, see Sidney Siegal, *Nonparametric Statistics for the Behavioral Sciences* (New York: McGraw-Hill, 1956).

25. For further discussion of Sunset legislation as an innovation, see Bruce Adams and Betsy Sherman, "Sunset Implementation: A Positive Partnership to Make Government Work," *Public Administration Review* 38 (January/February 1978): 78–81; and William M. Pearson and Van A. Wigginton, "Effectiveness of Administrative Controls: Some Perceptions of State Legislators," *Public Administration Review* 46 (July/August 1986): 328–331.

26. In this discriminant analysis, Hamm and Robertson's dichotomous dependent variable was adoption/nonadoption of Sunset legislation. Their independent variables were: estimated legislative compensation, 1971–78; percentage legislators returned to office between 1971 and 1976; the mean number of appointments the legislature had control over from 1968 to 1978; an indicator of existing program review; an occupational licensing score; the mean number of full-time state employees; a veto index; and a divided party control score. See Keith E.

Hamm and Roby D. Robertson, "Factors Influencing the Adoption of New Methods of Legislative Oversight in the U.S. States," *Legislative Studies Quarterly* 1, no. 1 (February 1981): 133–150.

27. Walker, "Diffusion of Innovations," p. 886.

28. Common Cause, *Status of Sunset*, p. 25.

Chapter 4

1. Peter deLeon provides an outline of his framework in two of his manuscripts: "Public Policy Termination: An End and a Beginning," *Policy Analysis* 4 (1978): 379–386; and "A Theory of Policy Termination," in *The Policy Cycle*, ed. Judith V. May and Aaron B. Wildavsky (Beverly Hills, CA: Sage, 1978), pp. 286–292.

2. This particular termination theory of Herbert Kaufman is found in: *Time, Chance and Organizations: Natural Selection in a Perilous Environment* (Chatham, NJ: Chatham House, 1985), pp. 144–146.

3. Angela Crawford, "Lawyer Says Progress on Teen Justice in Peril," *Tulsa World*, May 27, 1990, p. A4.

4. Ibid.

5. Ibid.

6. Ibid., p. A1.

7. Robert Hoover, "Task Force Examining State's Juvenile Justice System," *Tulsa World*, November 6, 1990, p. A1.

8. Robert D. Behn, "Closing the Massachusetts Public Training Schools," *Policy Sciences* 7, no. 2 (June 1976): 151–171.

9. Ibid., pp. 156–158. For examples of behavioral research in this field, see La Mar T. Empey, "Alternatives to Incarceration," in *Delinquency and Social Policy*, ed. Paul Lerman (New York: Praeger, 1970); and George Mora, Max Talmadge, Francis T. Bryant, and Benjamin S. Hayden, "A Residential Treatment Center Moves Toward the Community Mental Health Model," in *Residential Treatment of Emotionally Disturbed Children*, ed. George H. Weber and Bernard J. Haberlein (New York: Behavioral Publications, 1972), pp. 227–239.

10. Crawford, "Lawyer Says Progress on Teen Justice in Peril," pp. A1, A4.

11. Angela Crawford, "Walters Dislikes DHS Juvenile Plan," *Tulsa World*, February 14, 1989, p. A1.

12. Marty Beyer, Paul DeMuro, and Ira Schwartz, *Comprehensive Services for Oklahoma's Delinquent, Deprived, in Need of Treatment, and in Need of Services Children: Final Report* (Oklahoma City, 1990), p. 15.

13. Ibid., p. 16.

14. The national standard ratio of psychiatric beds to population, recommended by the National Institutes of Mental Health (NIMH), is two beds for every 10,000 children (Beyer et al., *Comprehensive Services*, p. 27). Applied to Oklahoma in 1990, this results in a recommendation of 180 beds. In fact, there were 1,810 psychiatric beds available in Oklahoma for the treatment of children and adolescents, more than ten times the number recommended by NIMH.

15. For a longer discussion about the recent popularity and treatment effectiveness of children's psychiatric hospitals, see Mark R. Daniels, "The Politics

and Economics of Dependent Children's Mental Health Care Financing: The Oklahoma Paradox," *Journal of Health and Human Services Administration* 16 (1993): 171–196.

16. George A. Miller, deputy director of the Department of Human Services, State of Oklahoma, Personal Interview, March 12, 1994.

17. William Booth, "Committed Youth," *Newsweek*, July 31, 1989, pp. 66–69, 72.

18. Beyer et al., *Comprehensive Services*, p. 7.

19. See Daniels, "Politics and Economics."

20. Beyer et al., *Comprehensive Services*, pp. iv-x.

21. See Behn, "Closing the Massachusetts Public Training Schools."

22. Richard Kilgore, "One Children's Mental Health Bill Approved While Another Fails," *Tulsa World*, March 13, 1991, p. A1.

23. Vincent Eastman, "More Secure Space Needed, Panel Says," *Tulsa World*, August 4, 1990, pp. A4, A14.

24. Robert Hoover, "Location of 'Terry D.' Not Known, Says Attorney Who Filed Suit," *Tulsa World*, December 11, 1990, p. A4.

Chapter 5

1. Robert D. Behn, "How to Terminate a Public Policy: A Dozen Hints for the Would-be Terminator," *Policy Analysis 4*, no. 3 (Summer 1978): 393–413.

2. James M. Hoefler and Khi V. Thai, "Introduction to Politics and Economics of Health Care Finance: A Symposium," *Journal of Health and Human Services Administration* 16, no. 2 (1993): 115–120.

3. Department of Finance and Administration, *TennCare: New Direction in Health Care* (Nashville: State of Tennessee, 1993).

4. U.S. Bureau of the Census, *Current Population Survey* (Washington, DC: Government Printing Office, 1994).

5. Hoefler and Thai, "Politics and Economics of Health Care Finance."

6. Ibid.

7. Ibid.

8. J.A. Lee, "A Primer on Managed Care," *Journal of Health and Human Services Administration* 16, no. 2 (1993): 144–156.

9. Department of Finance and Administration, *Medicaid: Tennessee's Health Care Problem* (Nashville: State of Tennessee, 1993).

10. Jeffrey L. Pressman and Aaron B. Wildavsky, *Implementation* (Berkeley: University of California Press, 1973).

11. Tennessee Medical Association, *TennCare Alert*, no. 8 (January 26, 1994).

12. Personal Interview with Mark Greene, executive director, Tennessee Medical Association, January 10, 1994.

13. Ed Cromer and Bill Snyder, "Doctors Deluged by TennCare Calls," *Nashville Banner*, October 8, 1993, p. A1.

14. Chris Sherrill Vass, "Doctor Asks Governor to Take Cuts and See How He Likes It," *Chattanooga News-Free Press*, November 5, 1993, p. A2.

15. Tennessee Medical Association, *TennCare Alert*, no. 8 (January 26, 1994).

16. Jeff Woods, "TennCare: Banner Publisher Thinks Blue Cross Abusing Its

Power," *Nashville Banner*, November 9, 1993, p. A1.

17. Ed Cromer, "McWherter Says It's Time Feds Decide on TennCare," *Nashville Banner*, November 10, 1993, p. B1.

18. Rebecca Ferrar, "Governor Says US Delay in OK for TennCare Nears Critical Point," *Knoxville News-Sentinel*, October 13, 1993, p. A7.

19. Reed Branson, "State to Play Politics for TennCare Waiver," *Commercial Appeal*, October 13, 1993, p. A2.

20. Woods, "TennCare."

21. Reed Branson and James W. Brosman, "Reduce TennCare Gets Federal OK." *Commercial Appeal*, March 2, 1993, p. A1.

22. Jon Hamilton, "TennCare Switch Spells Distress to Many in Need," *Commercial Appeal*, January 5, 1994, p. B2.

23. Department of Finance and Administration, *Medicaid: Tennessee's Health Care Problem* (Nashville: State of Tennessee, 1993).

24. James W. Brosman, "Study Says Health Plan Will Save Tenn. Billions," *Commercial Appeal*, November 2, 1994, p. A4.

25. Ferrar, "Governor Says."

26. Michael Finn, "Governor Warned on Waiver Tactics," *Chattanooga News-Free Press*, November 9, 1993, p. 2.

27. Ed Cromer and Bill Snyder, "McWherter Takes Case for TennCare to Clinton," *Nashville Banner*, November 9, 1993, p. A1.

28. Duren Cheek, "Health-Plan Summit Slated," *The Tennessean*, February 3, 1994, p. B1.

29. Mark R. Daniels and James M. Regens, "Physicians' Assistants as a Health Care Delivery Mechanism: Incidence and Correlates of State Authorization," *Policy Studies Journal* 9, no. 2 (1981): A2.

30. Paula Wade, "Leave TennCare Alone, McWherter Implores Bill-Happy Lawmakers," *Chattanooga News-Free Press*, November 5, 1993, p. A2.

31. Nashville Bureau, "TennCare Reform Sponsor Decries Death of Last Bill," *Commercial Appeal*, April 6, 1994, p. A8.

32. Hamilton, "TennCare Switch Spells Distress."

33. Ibid.

34. Associated Press, "Baby Death, TennCare Link Probed," *Commercial Appeal*, February 19, 1994, p. A8.

35. Anna Byrd Davis, "Move to TennCare Reduced Eye, Dental Services to Poor," *Commercial Appeal*, March 17, 1994, p. A1.

36. Richard Locker, "TennCare Problems Examined at Hearing," *Commercial Appeal*, March 1, 1994, p. B1.

Chapter 6

1. Peter deLeon, "A Theory of Policy Termination," in *The Policy Cycle*, ed. Judith V. May and Aaron B. Wildavsky (Beverly Hills, CA: Sage, 1978), pp. 279–300.

2. Peter deLeon, "Policy Termination as a Political Phenomenon," in *The Politics of Program Evaluation*, ed. Dennis Palumbo (Newbury Park, CA: Sage, 1987), pp. 173–199.

3. Janet E. Frantz, "The High Cost of Policy Termination," *International Journal of Public Administration* 20, no. 12 (1997).

4. Mitchell B. Wallerstein, "Terminating Entitlements: Veterans' Disability Benefits in the Depression," *Policy Sciences* 7, no. 2 (June 1976): 173–182.

5. Abram N. Shulsky, "Abolishing the District of Columbia Motorcycle Squad," *Policy Sciences* 7, no. 2 (June 1976): 183–197.

6. Peter deLeon, "Public Policy Termination: An End and a Beginning," *Policy Analysis* 4 (1978): 379–386; idem, "A Theory of Policy Termination," pp. 286–292.

7. Janet E. Frantz, "Reviving and Revising a Termination Model," *Policy Sciences* 25 (1992): 175–189.

8. Michael Harris, "Policy Termination: Uncovering the Ideological Dimension," *International Journal of Public Administration* 20, no. 12 (1997).

9. Robert D. Behn, "Closing the Massachusetts Public Training Schools," *Policy Sciences* 7, no. 2 (June 1976): 151–171; and Mark R. Daniels, "Organizational Termination and Policy Continuation: Closing the Oklahoma Public Training Schools," *Policy Sciences* 28, no. 2 (June 1995): 301–316.

10. For Behn's dozen hints, see Robert D. Behn, "How to Terminate a Public Policy: A Dozen Hints for the Would-be Terminator," *Policy Analysis* 4, no. 3 (Summer 1978): 393–413.

11. James M. Cameron, "Ideology and Policy Termination: Restructuring California's Mental Health System," in May and Wildavsky, eds., *The Policy Cycle*, pp. 301–328.

12. deLeon, "Policy Termination as a Political Phenomenon."

13. Eugene Bardach's categorization of termination advocates is discussed fully in chapter 2.

14. Justin Greenwood, "The Succession of Policy Termination," *International Journal of Public Administration* 20, no. 12 (1997).

15. Shulsky, "Abolishing the District of Columbia Motorcycle Squad."

16. Wallerstein, "Terminating Entitlements."

17. deLeon, 1978, "A Theory of Policy Termination."

18. Frantz, "Reviving and Revising."

19. Dorothy Norris-Tirrell, "Organization Termination in the Nonprofit Setting: The Dissolution of Children's Rehabilitation Services," *International Journal of Public Administration* 20, no. 12 (1997).

20. Keith J. Mueller, "Federal Programs to Expire: The Case of Health Planning," *Public Administration Review* 48, no. 3 (May/June 1988): 719–725.

21. Norris-Tirrell, "Organization Termination."

22. Richard Chackerian, "Reorganization of State Governments: 1900–1985," *Journal of Public Administration Research and Theory* 6, no. 1 (January 1996): 25–47.

23. Samuel Best, Paul Teske, and Michael Mintrom, "Terminating the Oldest Living Regulator: The Death of the Interstate Commerce Commission," *International Journal of Public Administration* 20, no. 12 (1997).

24. David Osborne and Ted Gaebler, *Reinventing Government: How the Entrepreneurial Spirit Is Transforming the Public Sector* (New York: Penguin, 1993).

25. Daniel Tarschys, "The Scissors Crisis in Public Finance," *Policy Sciences* 15 (1983): 205–224.

26. Robert Behn, "Closing a Government Facility," *Public Administration Review* 38, no. 4 (1978): 332–338.

27. Robert P. Biller, "On Tolerating Policy and Organizational Termination: Some Design Considerations," *Policy Sciences* 7, no. 2 (June 1976): 133–149.

28. Eugene Bardach, "Policy Termination as a Political Process." *Policy Sciences* 7 no. 2 (June 1976): 123.

Bibliography

Books and Monographs

Beyer, Marty, Paul DeMuro, and Ira Schwartz. *Comprehensive Services for Oklahoma's Delinquent, Deprived, In Need of Treatment, and in Need of Services Children: Final Report*. Oklahoma City, 1990.

Brewer, Garry, and Peter deLeon. *The Foundations of Policy Analysis*. Homewood, IL: Dorsey Press, 1983.

Common Cause. *The Status of Sunset in the States: A Common Cause Report*. Washington, DC: Common Cause, 1982.

Department of Finance and Administration. *TennCare: New Direction in Health Care*. Nashville: State of Tennessee, 1993.

————. *Medicaid: Tennessee's Health Care Problem*. Nashville: State of Tennessee, 1993.

Gore, Al. *Creating a Government That Works Better and Costs Less*. New York: Plume/Penguin, 1993.

Jones, Charles O. *An Introduction to the Study of Public Policy*. Monterey, CA: Brooks Cole, 1984.

Kaufman, Herbert. *Are Government Organizations Immortal?*. Washington, DC: Brookings, 1976.

————. *Time, Chance and Organizations: Natural Selection in a Perilous Environment*. Chatham, NJ: Chatham House, 1987.

Levine, Charles H. *Managing Fiscal Stress: The Crisis in the Public Sector*. Chatham, NJ: Chatham House, 1980.

————. *The Politics of Retrenchment*. Beverly Hills, CA: Sage, 1982.

Osborne, David, and Ted Gaebler. *Reinventing Government: How the Entrepreneurial Spirit Is Transforming the Public Sector*. New York: Plume/Penguin, 1993.

Pressman, Jeffrey L., and Aaron B. Wildavsky. *Implementation*. Berkeley: University of California Press, 1973.

Siegal, Sidney. *Nonparametric Statistics for the Behavioral Sciences*. New York: McGraw-Hill, 1956.

Simon, Herbert A., Donald W. Smithburg, and Victor A. Thompson. *Public Administration*. New York: Knopf, 1950.

U.S. Bureau of the Census. *Current Population Survey*. Washington, DC: Government Printing Office, 1994.

Chapters in Edited Volumes

Cameron, James M. "Ideology and Policy Termination: Restructuring California's Mental Health System." In *The Policy Cycle*, ed. Judith V. May and Aaron B. Wildavsky, pp. 301–328. Beverly Hills, CA: Sage, 1978.

Daniels, Mark R. "Terminating Bureaucracy: Ending Public Programs, Policies and Organizations." In *Handbook of Bureaucracy*, ed. Ali Farazmand, pp. 446–466. New York: Marcel Dekker, 1994.

deLeon, Peter, "Policy Termination as a Political Phenomenon," In *The Politics of Program Evaluation*, ed. Dennis Palumbo, pp. 173–199. Newbury Park, CA: Sage, 1987.

———. "A Theory of Policy Termination." In May and Wildavsky, eds., *The Policy Cycle*, pp. 173–199.

Empey, La Mar T. "Alternatives to Incarceration." In *Delinquency and Social Policy*, ed. Paul Lerman, New York: Praeger, 1970.

Mora, George, Max Talmadge, Francis T. Bryant, and Benjamin S. Hayden, "A Residential Treatment Center Moves toward the Community Mental Health Model." In *Residential Treatment of Emotionally Disturbed Children*, ed. George H. Weber and Bernard J. Haberlein, pp. 227–239. New York: Behavioral Publications, 1972.

Journal Articles

Adams, Bruce, and Betsy Sherman. "Sunset Implementation: A Positive Partnership to Make Government Work." *Public Administration Review* 38 January/February 1978): 78–81.

Bardach, Eugene. "Policy Termination as a Political Process." *Policy Sciences* 7, no. 2 (June 1976): 123–131.

Behn Robert D. "Closing the Massachusetts Public Training Schools." *Policy Sciences* 7, no. 2 (June 1976): 151–171.

———. "How to Terminate a Public Policy: A Dozen Hints for the Would-be Terminator." *Policy Analysis* 4, no. 3 (Summer 1978): 393–413.

———. "Closing a Government Facility." *Public Administration Review* 38, no. 4 (1978): 332–338.

———. "The False Dawn of Sunset Laws." *Public Interest* 49 (Fall 1977): 103–118.

Best, Samuel, Paul Teske, and Michael Mintrom. "Terminating the Oldest Living Regulator: The Death of the Interstate Commerce Commission." *International Journal of Public Administration* 20 (1997).

Biller, Robert P. "On Tolerating Policy and Organizational Termination: Some Design Considerations." *Policy Sciences* 7, no. 2 (June 1976): 133–149.

Bradley, Valerie J. "Policy Termination in Mental Health: The Hidden Agenda." *Policy Sciences* 7, no. 2 (June 1976): 215–224.

Brewer, Garry. "Termination: Hard Choices, Harder Questions." *Public Administration Review* 38 (1978): 338–344.

Chackerian, Richard. "Reorganization of State Governments: 1900–1985." Manuscript, Askew School of Public Administration and Policy, Florida State University, May 24, 1995.

Daniels, Mark R. "Theories for the Termination of Public Programs, Policies and Organizations." *International Journal of Public Administration* 20, no. 12 (1997).

———. "Implementing Policy Termination: Health Care Reform in Tennessee." *Policy Studies Review* 14 no. 3/4 (Autumn/Winter 1996): 353–374.

———. "Organizational Termination and Policy Continuation: Closing the Oklahoma Public Training Schools." *Policy Sciences* 28, no. 2 (June 1995): 301–316.

———. "Termination, Innovation and the American States: Testing Sunset Legislation." *American Review of Politics* 15 (Winter 1995): 507–518.

———. "The Politics and Economics of Dependent Children's Mental Health Care Financing: The Oklahoma Paradox." *Journal of Health and Human Services Administration* 16 (1993): 171–196.

Daniels, Mark R., and James M. Regens. "Physicians' Assistants as a Health Care Delivery Mechanism: Incidence and Correlates of State Authorization." *Policy Studies Journal* 9, no. 2 (1981): 242–249.

deLeon, Peter. "Policy Evaluation and Program Termination." *Policy Studies Review* 2, no. 4 (May 1983): 631–647.

———. "Public Policy Termination: An End and A Beginning." *Policy Analysis* 4 (1978): 369–392.

———. "Afterward: The Once and Future State of Policy Termination." *International Journal of Public Administration* 20, no. 12 (1997).

Ellis, Carol L. "Program Termination: A Word to the Wise." *Public Administration Review* 43, no. 4 (1983): 352–357.

Foster, James L., and Garry D. Brewer. "And the Clocks Were Striking Thirteen: The Termination of War." *Policy Sciences* 7, no. 2 (June 1976): 225–243.

Frantz, Janet E. "Reviving and Revising a Termination Model." *Policy Sciences* 25 (1992): 175–189.

———. "The High Cost of Policy Termination." *International Journal of Public Administration* 20, no. 12 (1997).

Gray, Virginia. "Innovation in the States: A Diffusion Study." *American Political Science Review* 67 (1973): 1174–1185.

Greenwood, Justin. "The Succession of Policy Termination." *International Journal of Public Administration* 20, no. 12 (1997).

Hamm, Keith E., and Roby D. Robertson. "Factors Influencing the Adoption of New Methods of Legislative Oversight in the U.S. States." *Legislative Studies Quarterly* 1, no. 1 (1981): 133–150.

Harris, Michael. "Policy Termination: Uncovering the Ideological Dimension." *International Journal of Public Administration* 20, no. 12 (1997).

Hines, Samuel M. "Organizations and Evolution: A Review of Herbert Kaufman's *Time, Chance, and Organizations." Politics and the Life Sciences* 5 (1987): 266.

Hoefler, J.M., and K.V. Thai. "Introduction to Politics and Economics of Health Care Finance: A Symposium." *Journal of Health and Human Services Administration* 16, no. 2 (1993): 115–120.

Katzenbach, Edward L. "The Horse Calvary in the Twentieth Century: A Study of Policy Response." *Public Policy* 8 (1958): 120–149.

Kearney, Richard C. "Sunset: A Survey and Analysis of the State Experience." *Public Administration Review* 50 (January/February 1990): 49–57.

Lambright, W. Henry, and Harvey M. Sapolsky. "Terminating Federal Research and Development Programs." *Policy Sciences* 7, no. 2 (June 1976): 199–213.

Lee, J.A. "A Primer on Managed Care." *Journal of Health and Human Resources Administration* 16, no. 2 (1993): 144–156.

Mueller, Keith J. "Federal Programs to Expire: The Case of Health Planning." *Public Administration Review* 48, no. 3 (May/June 1988): 719–725.

Norris-Tirrell, Dorothy. "Organization Termination in the Nonprofit Setting: The Dissolution of Children's Rehabilitation Services." *International Journal of Public Administration* 20, no. 12 (1997).

Pearson, William M., and Van A. Wigginton. "Effectiveness of Administrative Controls: Some Perceptions of State Legislators." *Public Administration Review* 46 (July/August 1986): 328–331.

Savage, Robert L. "Policy Innovativeness as a Trait of American States." *Journal of Politics* 40 (1978): 212–224.

Shulsky, Abram N. "Abolishing the District of Columbia Motorcycle Squad." *Policy Sciences* 7, no. 2 (June 1976): 183–197.

Tarschys, Daniel. "The Scissors Crisis in Public Finance." *Policy Sciences* 15 (1983): 205–224.

Wade, Nicholas. "Death of the B-1: The Events Behind Carter's Decision." *Science* 197 (August 5, 1977): 536–539.

Walker, Jack L. "The Diffusion of Innovations among the American States." *American Political Science Review* 63 (1969): 880–899.

Wallerstein, Mitchel B. "Terminating Entitlements: Veterans' Disability Benefits in the Depression." *Policy Sciences* 7, no. 2 (June 1976): 173–182.

White, Elliot. "A Review of *Time, Chance and Organizations." Politics and the Life Sciences* 5 (1987): 268.

Newspapers and Magazines

Associated Press. "Baby Death, TennCare Link Probed." *Commercial Appeal,* February 19, 1994, p. A8.

Booth, William. "Committed Youth." *Newsweek,* July 31, 1989, pp. 66–69, 72.

Branson, Reed. "State to Play Politics for TennCare Waiver." *Commercial Appeal,* October 13, 1993, p. A2.

Branson, Reed, and James W. Brosman. "Reduced TennCare Gets Federal OK." *Commercial Appeal,* March 2, 1993, p. A1.

Brosman, James W. "Study Says Health Plan Will Save Tenn. Billions." *Commercial Appeal,* March 2, 1994, p. A4.

Cheek, Duren. "Health-Plan Summit Slated." *The Tennessean*, February 3, 1994, p. B1.

Crawford, Angela. "Lawyer Says Progress on Teen Justice in Peril." *Tulsa World*, May 27, 1990, p. A4.

————. "Walters Dislikes DHS Juvenile Plan." *Tulsa World*, February 14, 1989, p. A1.

Cromer, Ed. "McWherter Says It's Time Feds Decide on TennCare." *Nashville Banner*, November 10, 1993, p. B1.

Cromer, Ed, and Bill Synder. "Doctors Deluged by TennCare Calls." *Nashville Banner*, October 8, 1993, p. A1.

————. "McWherter Takes Case for TennCare to Clinton." *Nashville Banner*, November 9, 1993, p. A1.

Davis, Anna Byrd. "Move to TennCare Reduced Eye, Dental Services to Poor." *Commercial Appeal*, March 17, 1994, p. A1.

Eastman, Vincent. "More Secure Space Needed, Panel Says." *Tulsa World*, August 4, 1990, pp. A4, A14.

Ferrar, Rebecca. "Governor Says U.S. Delay in OK for TennCare Nears Critical Point." *Knoxville News-Sentinel*, October 13, 1993, p. A7.

Finn, Michael. "Governor Warned on Waiver Tactics." *Chattanooga News-Free Press*, November 9, 1993, p. A1.

Hamilton, Jon. "TennCare Switch Spells Distress to Many in Need." *Commercial Appeal*, January 5, 1994, p. B2.

Hoover, Dwayne. "Task Force Examining State's Juvenile Justice System." *Tulsa World*, November 6, 1990, p. A1.

————. "Location of 'Terry D.' Not Known, Says Attorney Who Filed Suit." *Tulsa World*, December 11, 1990, p. A4.

Kilgore, Richard T. "One Children's Mental Health Bill Approved While Another Fails." *Tulsa World*, March 13, 1991, p. A1.

Locker, Richard. "TennCare Problems Examined at Hearing." *Commercial Appeal*, March 1, 1994, p. B1.

Nashville Bureau. "TennCare Reform Sponsor Decries Death of Last Bill." *Commercial Appeal*, April 6, 1994, p. A8.

Tennessee Medical Association. *TennCare Alert*, no. 8, January 26, 1994.

Vass, Chris Sherrill. "Doctor Asks Governor to Take Cuts and See How He Likes It." *Chattanooga News-Free Press*, November 5, 1993, p. A2.

Wade, Paula. "Leave TennCare Alone, McWherter Implores Bill-Happy Lawmakers." *Chattanooga News-Free Press,* November 5, 1993, p. A2.

Woods, Jeff. "TennCare: Banner Publisher Thinks Blue Cross Abusing Its Power." *Nashville Banner*, November 9, 1993, p. A1.

Interviews

Greene, Mark, executive director, Tennessee Medical Association, January 10, 1994.

Miller, George A., deputy director of the Department of Human Services, State of Oklahoma, March 12, 1994.

Index

Mark R. Daniels is associate professor of government and public affairs and coordinator of the Master of Public Administration program at Slippery Rock University of Pennsylvania. He received his Ph.D. in political science from the University of Georgia and has served on the faculties of several universities, including Oklahoma State University and the University of Connecticut. An author of over thirty articles and book chapters, he has served as editor of the symposium "Public Policy and Organization Termination" (*International Journal of Public Administration,* Fall 1997) and of the book *Medicaid Reform and the American States: Cases on the Politics of Managed Care* (1997). Dr. Daniels is an active member of the American Society for Public Administration (ASPA) and edits the newsletter of ASPA's Section on Public Administration Education, the *SPAE Forum.*